JACQUELINE BOUVIER KENNEDY

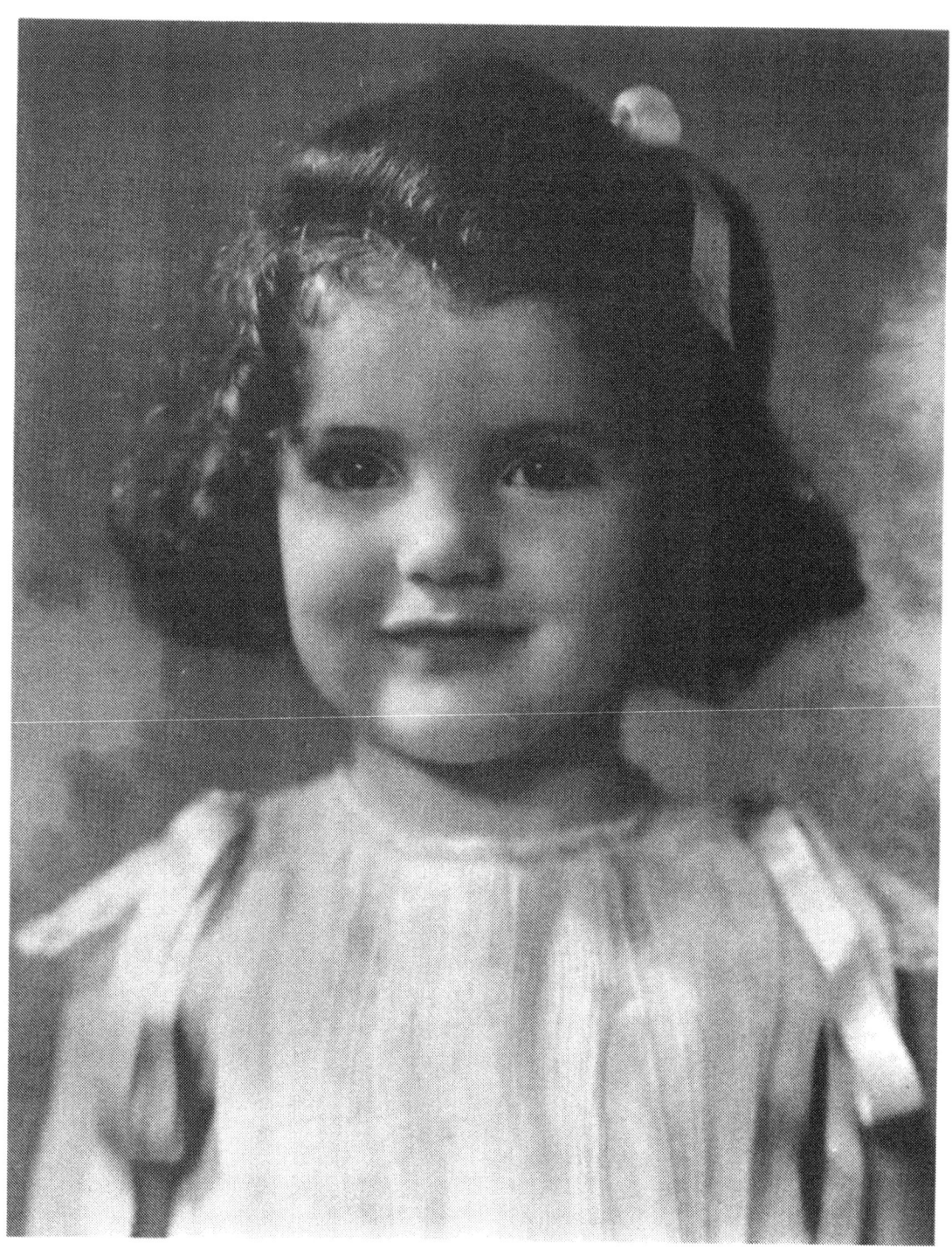

Formal portrait of Jacqueline Lee Bouvier, aged three, almost four.

JACQUELINE BOUVIER KENNEDY

MARY VAN RENSSELAER THAYER

DOUBLEDAY & COMPANY, INC.
GARDEN CITY, NEW YORK

Library of Congress Catalog Card Number 61-17432
Copyright © 1961 by Mary Van Rensselaer Thayer
All Rights Reserved
Printed in the United States of America

Part One

JACQUELINE LEE BOUVIER was not really a pretty baby. Instead of looking rosy, she looked peaked. She was six weeks late in arriving and somewhat unexpectedly chose to be born on a sunny Sunday afternoon in July. Plans had been made for the great event to take place in New York. But since both mother and doctor were weekending in their summer homes, there was a last-minute switch to the small, efficient hospital in nearby Southampton. She weighed eight pounds and seemed, understandably, more mature than most newborn babies.

Her mother was twenty-one. A brunette beauty with a lovely name, Janet Lee, she had been belle of her debutante season and, despite her smallness and appealing femininity, was one of the most skillful and daring horsewomen in the country.

The baby was named after her father, Jack Bouvier, whose full, distinguished name was John Vernou Bouvier III. He was thirty-seven, and until his marriage the previous year had been considered one of social New York's most irreconcilable bachelors. He was dark, in summers tanned to swarthiness, and so good-looking that friends nicknamed him The Sheik, while strangers were forever taking him for Clark Gable. Together, Mr. and Mrs. John Vernou Bouvier III were considered the handsomest couple on Long Island. Their daughter, Jacqueline, would start life with every asset.

Within a very short time baby Jacqueline began to blossom into a beauty. She possessed four teeth when she had aged as many months. She could talk, and really talk,

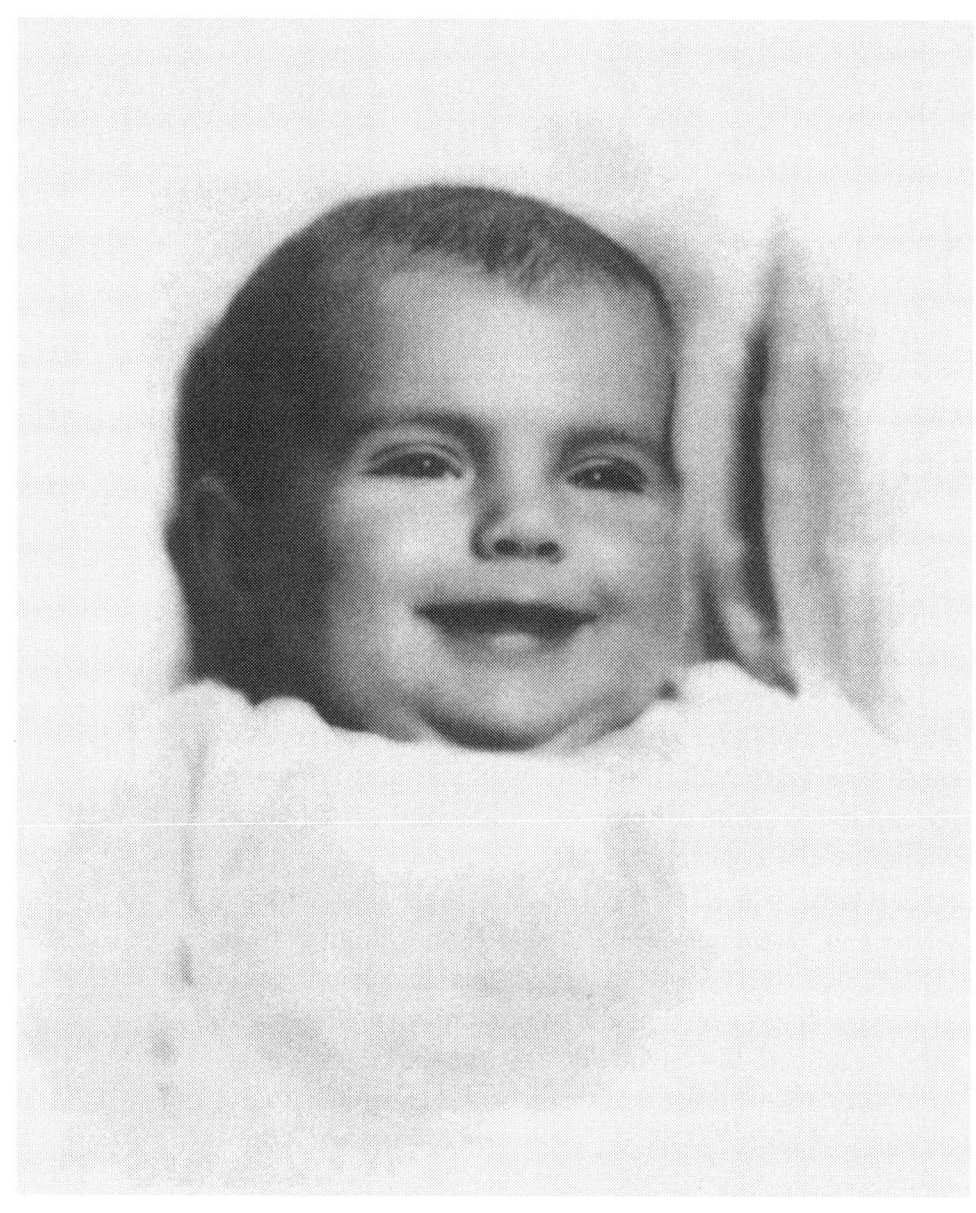

This first formal portrait of Jacqueline was made at the age of five months and shortly before her christening. She is wearing her grandfather's christening robe. Bought in Paris, it is fashioned of gossamer lawn and strewn with miniature hand-embroidered bouquets. Caroline Kennedy also wore this charming dress at her christening.

before she was a year old. All her loving relatives—two sets of grandparents, five aunts, an uncle, a dozen or so young cousins—agreed that she was an altogether remarkable child. When they dropped in to see the baby, they admired her fluff of faintly curling black hair, her newly rosy complexion, her wide eyes, all set off so coquettishly by the froufrou of peachy-pink point-d'esprit flounces on her beige wicker bassinet.

No one imagined, of course, that this placid infant would someday be the thirty-first First Lady of the land. Nor that the bassinet, now painted white and simply trimmed with ribbon-threaded dotted swiss, would cradle Jacqueline's look-alike son, John Fitzgerald Kennedy, Jr., the first White House baby in over half a century.

Three days before Christmas, Jacqueline Lee Bouvier was christened at the Church of St. Ignatius Loyola in New York. Her father's only brother, William Sergeant Bouvier, who was affectionately known as "Bud," had died in October and his almost ten-year-old son, Michel, acted as godfather. Jacqueline was dressed in an exquisite Paris creation first used at the christening of her maternal grandfather, James T. Lee. Three generations of babies, including Caroline Kennedy, have worn this charming christening robe. It is long-skirted, with puffed sleeves gathered at tiny wrists, and is fashioned of gossamer lawn, frilled with fine lace and strewn with miniature bouquets hand-embroidered in microscopic stitches.

Since early childhood Jack Bouvier had summered at East Hampton in the enormous lawn-and-garden-surrounded stucco Bouvier house. It was called Lasata, an Indian name meaning "Place of Peace," but was by far the liveliest spot in the neighborhood. There were five Bouvier sisters and brothers: Jack, Bud, Edith and the strawberry-blond twins, Maude and Michelle.

Janet Lee was in her early teens when the James T. Lees spent their first summer in East Hampton. She was second in a trio of attractive sisters, Marion, Janet, Winifred, who later were to cause considerable local excitement not only because of their charm but because each owned an automobile with a fancy, distinctive horn! The Bouvier twins were around Janet's age and they became friends. Their brother Jack was sixteen years older than Janet. A notable charmer and desirable matrimonial catch, he had no time to notice teen-age friends of his sisters.

Janet Lee was brought up in the Glittering Twenties like the daughters of many well-born, affluent New York parents. She went to Miss Spence's School, learned the social graces and studied two years at college (one at Sweet Briar, and another at Barnard). Besides, she developed an intuitive command over horses which was to carry her to the top rank of women riders. She grew prettier as the years passed and made her debut conventionally at a dance at Sherry's. It was the summer afterward that Jack Bouvier began to find time for his twin sisters' young friend.

On July 7, 1928, Janet and Jack Bouvier's wedding took place in St. Philomena's Church in East Hampton. The six bridesmaids wore jonquil-colored chiffon and green straw hats. The matron and maid of honor, sisters of the bride, reversed the color scheme with green chiffon and jonquil-yellow hats. It was all so perfect that a New York society reporter rapturized on her typewriter: "Have you ever glimpsed the loveliness of a bed of nodding green and gold jonquils in the sunshine? Surely you've all seen a stately bride bedecked in satin, lace and silver? Combine these effects and you'll have a glowing picture of Mrs. John Vernou Bouvier III, stepping into the sunshine

Janet Lee and John Vernou Bouvier III were married in St. Philomena's Church in East Hampton, July 7, 1928. A New York reporter described the new Mrs. Bouvier as a "stately bride bedecked in satin, lace and silver" and her bridesmaids "lovely as green and gold jonquils nodding in the sunshine." (IRA A. HILL)

from the door of quaint St. Philomena's Church yesterday with her attendants about her."

There were five hundred guests at the midday reception on the porches and lawns of the Lee house on Lily Pond Lane. Meyer Davis's orchestra played (as it played at the Inaugural Ball for President and Mrs. Kennedy). The couple sailed off on the *Aquitania.* All this was true to pattern in rosy, predepression years.

The newlyweds returned to a small, rented house in East Hampton, and when winter came moved to a New York apartment. A year after Jacqueline was born her grandfather, James T. Lee, gave his daughter Janet a duplex apartment in a Park Avenue property he owned. An ultraconservative, James Lee, who at eighty-four still works at his job as president of New York's Central Savings Bank, disliked the idea of a young couple with a child not having a permanent home.

Here, under the watchful eyes of her nurse, Bertha Newey, Jacqueline was growing up into an independent, strong-minded, pixily-humored, stubbornly honest, beguiling child. At two she made her press debut in the same role which less than three decades later she now plays in the White House.

It was her second birthday. Twenty little boys and girls were invited to her party. A society columnist reported the event: "Little Jackie Bouvier, daughter of Jack Bouvier and the former Janet Lee, will not make her bow to society for another sixteen years or more, but she was a charming hostess at her second birthday party given at the home of her parents, 'Rowdy Hall,' on Egypt Lane." The afternoon was spent in pony rides—for the hostess had already acquired assurance astride—and games. The festivities were polished off with a Jack Horner pie and birthday cake.

Hootchie, the Scotty pup, was Jacqueline Bouvier's first pet. She "showed" him at an East Hampton Dog Show when she was two and received complimentary press notices. In this photograph, taken in Central Park in 1932, Jacqueline wears a light blue coat trimmed with gray squirrel, matching leggings, a bonnet with a pink frill, and white gloves.

That same summer, Jacqueline widened her scope. At an East Hampton dog show in which her Grandmother Bouvier and Aunt Edith carried off blue ribbons with Observer, a police dog, and Spot, a setter, Jacqueline also "showed" an entry. He was her first pet, a shaggy black Scotty named Hootchie. Reporters, who had already become ubiquitous in her life, duly recorded the event: "Little two-year-old Jacqueline Bouvier toddled to the show platform and exhibited with great pride a wee Scotch terrier of about her own size!" The scribe was obviously feminine, for she added: "Mr. Bouvier is so deeply tanned with East Hampton sunburn that he much resembles one of those handsome Egyptians you see careening along in their Rolls-Royce cars in Cairo, in the land of the Nile!"

After the second Bouvier sister, Caroline Lee, was born in the spring of 1933, three-and-a-half year-old Jacqueline took her afternoon naps in the spare room. It was a big room which also served later as a playroom for the little girls and was furnished somewhat incongruously with a set of heavy satinwood furniture, an unpleasing wedding present which her mother had stained mahogany. Here Jacqueline kept her favorite stuffed animals and her beloved rag doll Sammy, which she always took to bed with her.

Her independence and courage were extraordinary in one who was still a baby. A favorite family tale pointing up her sturdy character happened when she was four. One day with her nurse and less-than-year-old sister, she had gone to play in Central Park. Her mother, at home, answered the telephone.

"We have a little girl here," said a strange masculine voice. "We can't understand her name, but she knows her telephone number. Could she be yours?"

"Mummy, Jackie and Lee" is the inscription Jacqueline wrote on this photograph taken with her mother and baby sister Caroline Lee Bouvier who was born March 3, 1933. The baby is now Princess Stanislas Radziwill and lives in London. (IRA A. HILL)

It was the police. Frantic, Mrs. Bouvier hurried to the station house to find Jacqueline, completely at ease, chatting with the lieutenant. "Hello, Mummy," she said casually.

The officer on the Central Park beat told the story. He had noticed a little girl, alone, walking unconcernedly down a path. She stepped up to him, looked him straight in the eye and stated firmly, "My nurse is lost."

Some time later the nurse was found—in a far from happy state. When she missed her charge, she left the littler girl in care of another nurse and commenced running up and down the paths, calling Jacqueline's name. As time passed and there was no sign of Jackie, she became convinced that the child had been kidnaped. She was the first of many nurses and French governesses to find coping with determined Jacqueline difficult indeed.

Though her imagination was so vivid that, for instance, she delighted in telling grownups that a brown bear lived in her bedroom, she refused to fib or even tactfully gild the lily when confronted with a fact or situation. To Jacqueline black was black and white altogether white.

Her younger sister Lee, however, was always polite and diplomatic. In the Bouvier apartment house a favorite elevator man, as serious as his name, Ernest, was endowed with a crest of blonde hair which jutted irrepressibly above his forehead. One afternoon baby Lee, toddling into the elevator, lisped, "Ernest, you look pritty today."

Ernest was clearing his throat to thank Miss Lee when Jacqueline confronted her tiny sister like a thundercloud. "How can you say such a thing, Lee? It isn't true. You know perfectly well that Ernest looks just like a rooster!"

Ernest, pink of face, dropped the elevator right down into the basement. (Caroline Kennedy has an imagination much like her mother's. A short time ago she announced

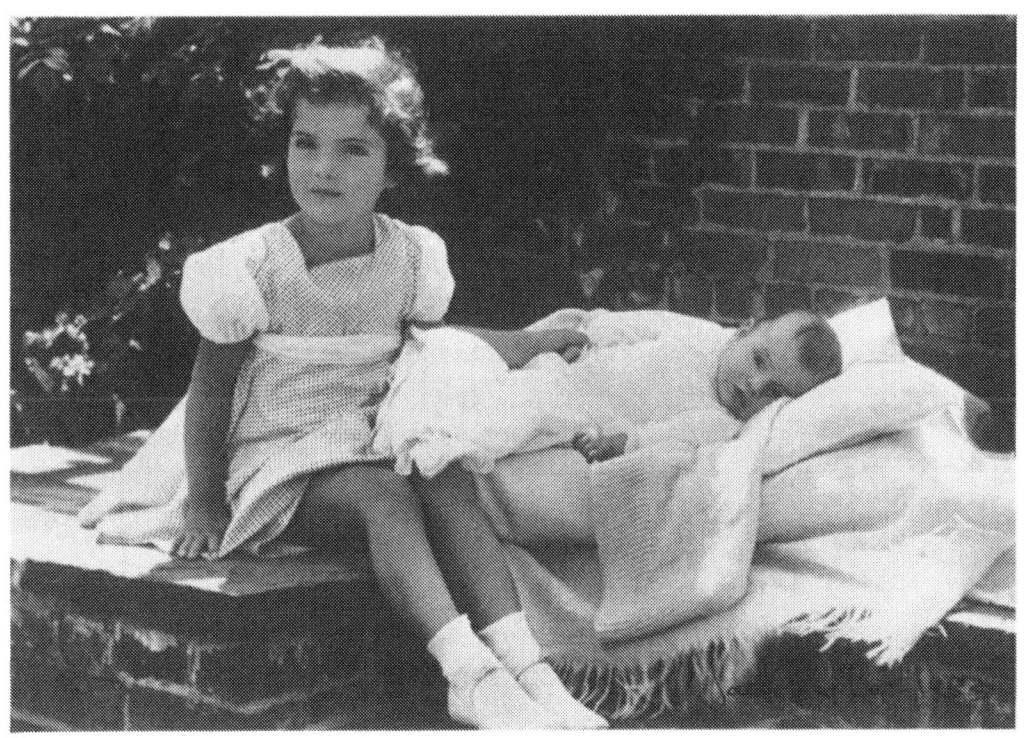

Jacqueline and Lee, three years younger, in the summer of 1933 at East Hampton, Long Island.

to her grandmother, "I just killed a wolf," adding gleefully, "I shot him." Just then grandmother Janet's white poodle, Charles of the Ritz, bounced into the room. "Oh! here's the wolf," exclaimed grandmother hopefully. "He's alive." "No," contradicted Caroline. "The wolf is black and he's hanging on the stairs.")

After a year of glorified kindergarten at Miss Yates's preschool class, Jacqueline went to Miss Chapin's School, a New York private school of long standing where three hundred or more daughters of well-to-do families and a sprinkling of exceptional scholarship students study hard; wear equalizing blue linen jumper uniforms; and are taught the precepts of good citizenship as well as the basic attributes of being a lady.

The school's headmistress was then Miss Ethel Stringfellow, and her ultimate task, in which she was most successful, was adjusting her girls to communal enterprise—or just plain getting along with one another. The most dreaded penalty, for those who were wicked, was to be despatched for a talk with the headmistress. To be sent to Miss Stringfellow once was a stigma hard to bear. To be sent often marked the culprit as an outlaw, yet added a delicious touch of distinction.

Jacqueline was an outlaw. Her brightness, almost precocity, made school too easy. She finished studying before her classmates, then found nothing but mischief to occupy her energies.

Even her mother didn't suspect the enormity of her daughter's sins until an afternoon when she was taking care of Jacqueline and a number of other little girls in Central Park. Jackie started acting up. "Isn't she a naughty little girl?" her mother said brightly to one of her daughter's small friends.

"Oh, yes," came the solemn, unexpected answer. "She's

Jacqueline was three when this photograph was made with her mother. (IRA A. HILL)

the very worst girl in school!" Then, relishing Janet's surprise, the friend added complacently, "Jackie does something bad every day. She gets sent to Miss Stringfellow every day—well, almost every day!"

Walking home from the park, Janet remarked casually, "Jackie, I hear you're sent to Miss Stringfellow very often."

The daughter glanced quickly at her mother, saw that she knew and nodded.

"What happens when you're sent to Miss Stringfellow?" Janet pursued.

"Well, I go to her office," commenced Jackie slowly, "and Miss Stringfellow says, 'Jacqueline, sit down. I've heard bad reports about you.' I sit down. Then Miss Stringfellow says a lot of things—but I don't listen."

Finally Miss Stringfellow found a way to attract Jacqueline's attention. She knew that her pupil was "mad" about horses. A Southerner who shared this interest, she said, in effect, "I know you love horses and you yourself are very much like a beautiful thoroughbred. You can run fast. You have staying power. You're well built and you have brains. But if you're not properly broken and trained, you'll be good for nothing. Suppose you owned the most beautiful race horse in the world. What good would he be if he wasn't trained to stay on the track, to stand still at the starting gate, to obey commands? He couldn't even pull a milk truck or a trash cart. He would be useless to you and you would have to get rid of him."

This was logic the young girl understood. Miss Stringfellow's mixture of firmness and understanding impressed Jacqueline, made her eager to please the headmistress and gain her respect. She ceased being a rebel. Without realizing it, she was becoming a leader. When she was grown Jacqueline liked to emphasize that Miss Stringfellow was "the first, great moral influence" in her life.

Some time later the sympathetic headmistress confided to Jacqueline's mother at one of the innumerable conferences about her daughter's progress and behavior, "I mightn't have kept Jacqueline—except that she has the most inquiring mind we've had in this school in thirty-five years!"

At home Jacqueline kept her books in a pair of bookcases her mother had given her as a Christmas present. She was partial to Beatrix Potter's *Peter Rabbit;* then breezed through *The Wizard of Oz's* dream world into the more sentimental saga of *Litle Lord Fauntleroy* and the endless goings on of *The Little Colonel.* She liked A. A. Milne and his *Winnie the Pooh,* too, and looked forward to Grandmother Bouvier's annual Christmas gift, usually delicious adventure stories like *The Far Distant Oxus.*

She possessed a fantastic memory which helped her learn to read very young. Her mother first realized the extent of her daughter's knowledge when she had reached the advanced age of six.

Books for grown-ups were kept in the guest room where Jacqueline took her afternoon naps. One day Jacqueline remarked offhandedly, "Mummy, I liked the story of the lady and the dog."

Her mother, puzzled, discovered that instead of sleeping, Jacqueline had been reading a book of short stories by Chekov. The plots were sophisticated and every character was labeled with an elaborate Russian name.

"Did you understand all the words?" asked Janet.

"Yes—except what's a midwife?" replied Jacqueline.

"Didn't you mind all those long names?" her mother persisted.

"No, why should I mind?" asked the six-year old logically.

Jacqueline had been scarcely a year old when she was first lifted astride a pony. As she grew bigger and stronger, with her mother or father at the other end of a lead line, she trotted and cantered on Rusty or Jerry, a pony and a miniature horse, which belonged to an East Hampton riding stable. She took to jumping fearlessly, sailing over low fences with great aplomb.

At five Jacqueline was a sufficiently assured equestrienne to ride on a hunter alongside her mother. That summer, the appealing pair, mounted on graceful, chestnut mares, won Third Prize in the Family Class at the East Hampton Horse Show. As a horsewoman, Jacqueline had something very fine to admire in her mother. Janet Bouvier not only rode her horses expertly but she also schooled them so perfectly and loved them so much, that they truly became family pets. Her most famous were three magnificent chestnuts—Stepaside, Clearanfast, Danseuse—and a bay mare named Arnoldean. For a decade she rode them in topflight horse shows throughout the East and at the National Horse Show, staged annually in New York's Madison Square Garden.

A slim, always impeccably habited figure, even blasé sportswriters described almost lyrically her expression as being as "determined as tennis champion Helen Wills Moody's when clearing difficult jumps and that once over and done, her dazzling smile was worth coming miles to see."

Both sports and social pages during the Thirties were filled with action shots of Mrs. Bouvier and her handsome mounts. Captions and headlines ran like this: "Here's a Picture of Grace and Skill"; "Mrs. Bouvier turns in perfect performance with hunter" at the National Horse Show; "Mrs. Bouvier has schooled the mare carefully and she gave a faultless exhibition"; "Mrs. Bouvier, riding

Riding with her mother in a Long Island show, Jacqueline, at five, already handled a good-sized horse competently. Mrs. Bouvier was one of the outstanding women riders in the East. (BERT & RICHARD MORGAN)

her mare Arnoldean, thrilled the audience with her performance over 8 foot, 4 inch jumps." On one of the rare times Danseuse faltered, a sportswriter complimented her: "... when Danseuse, a prime favorite—stumbled and threw her rider at a barrier—Mrs. Bouvier gave a remarkable exhibition of horsemanship when she courageously clung to the reins and retained control of the animal when prone."

Fashion writers, too, noted Janet Bouvier's sartorial perfection. As part of a winning three-man hunt team, she was photographed holding a silver trophy; "... she wears the very smartest in riding habits at Long Island horse shows. She's shown here in complete costume: Top hat, Ascot tie, coat with contrasting collar and trousers to match the collar. Long leather boots, of course."

When Jacqueline was six she was entered in a jumping class at the Southampton Horse Show. She was to be all on her own without a lead line. The other entrants were mostly children of ten, eleven, or twelve.

Her mother told her to go at the fences straight; the pony couldn't make it if he went in crooked. Janet sat in the grandstand, heart in mouth, as Jacqueline larruped first time around the ring, kicking her mount lustily to lift him over the jumps. Next time around, Jackie came whoopsing in crooked. The pony ducked and off she tumbled. Before anyone could get to her she bobbed right up. Furiously, she was trying to scramble back into the saddle on the wrong side when a horse-show official reached her.

The spectators, amused by the spunky little kid, broke into a roar of applause. Jacqueline, who never missed a trick, took note of the clapping. Motoring home, she suddenly turned to her mother. "Mummy, why did they clap when I fell off?"

Jacqueline, five, shows her annoyance at having been beaten in a lead-line class at a Smithtown, Long Island, show. She is leading her dispirited pony, Buddy, away from defeat. (BERT & RICHARD MORGAN)

Poem written by Jacqueline Bouvier at ten. She permitted reproduction of verses to show that, as a child, horses were not her sole interest.

Hastily Janet pulled the car over to the side of the road. "Those were terribly silly people," she said sternly, "they didn't know what really happened. You should be ashamed of handling your pony so carelessly. He might have been hurt." Jacqueline subsided quietly.

When Jacqueline wasn't riding, she was a tiny, absorbed railsitter at every horse show. She was usually close to her handsome father who, though he seldom rode, thoroughly appreciated horses and never missed a show. At seven, a photographer notes beneath her picture that "she has earned the distinction of being Long Island's youngest horse show fan—too young now to rival her mother's feats in the equine world, the promising young rider has been a spectator at every important contest for several seasons. Just mention the various horse shows," the caption continues, "and little Jackie can reel off the winners in every class."

At eight, pigtails flying, the camera catches her "showing very good form for a youngster as she canters her father's mount." That summer, at the Southampton Horse Show, against stiff competition, she was winner in the class for Children under Nine. Three years later she won the two prizes most sought after by young riders, the A.S.P.C.A. (American Society for Prevention of Cruelty of Animals) Alfred Maclay Trophy for Horsemanship and the A.S.P.C.A. Good Hands event. Both are national championships competed for in preliminary contests staged at various summer horse shows. The winners are eligible to enter the formal runoff at the Madison Square Garden Show.

There were twenty young contestants, boys and girls, at the finals. "Jacqueline Bouvier, an eleven year old equestrienne from East Hampton, Long Island, scored a double victory in the horsemanship competition," recorded the New York *Times*. "Miss Bouvier achieved a rare distinction," the newspaper applauded. "The occasions are few when a young rider wins both contests in the same show."

When Jacqueline was twelve or thirteen, serious, erect, competent, she was riding Ladies' Hunters. After the ponies and Jerry, the "compact" sized horse, there was an engaging, black-and-white piebald named Dancestep in Jacqueline's life. But the horse that was most beloved was her mother's famous chestnut hunter, Danseuse, the Virginia-born mare sired by Runantel out of Graceful Carrie. Danseuse won innumerable championships and they owned her twenty years.

Dignified John Vernou Bouvier, Jr., whom Jacqueline and Lee called Grampy Jack, pretended to take a dim view of the brilliant horsemanship which his daughter-in-law and granddaughter displayed. "Hrrrrumph, my girl!" he would say to Janet. "What would happen to your children if you fall and break your neck?" Nevertheless, he perked with pride when either won a prize and, since they won with almost monotonous regularity, it is reasonable to believe that the distinguished lawyer was in a constant glow.

When Jacqueline was fifteen, she became a first-year student at Miss Porter's School in Farmington, Connecticut, where many girls kept their own horses. She longed to take along Danseuse. The mare's keep would cost twenty-five dollars a month. Her family did not encourage this extravagance which she personally could not afford. So she wrote her grandfather asking if he would stand treat and, to sweeten the request, enclosed her newest poem for his criticism.

Mr. Bouvier replied in characteristically elegant style:

Dear Jacqueline:

What in one aspect might be viewed as a sumptuary extravagance may, on the other hand, from the mental and physical standpoint, be regarded as a justifiable necessity.

Within this generalization naturally falls Danseuse. Psychologically she aids you. Spiritually she provides a wholesome release from sordid worldly cares. Therefore will I engage to meet her keep of $25 a month until April next.

Are you or am I in these dreadful days justified in such an indulgence? I think not, but with the necessity for maintaining Danseuse both of us are in concurrence.

Affectionately,
Grandad.

Soon after the mare arrived Jacqueline wrote home: "Every day since Donny came I've gone up and groomed her and last night I went up to see her before the lecture. And Sue (her roommate) locked me in the stall with her. I was practically late but it was so much fun. She (Donny) is very happy in a box stall between two horses whom she kisses through the bars and she is wearing a stolen blanket which I snitched from another horse!"

That first rugged Connecticut winter Donny, too, learned a lot. Patiently, ingeniously, Jacqueline trained the adaptable showring mare to pull a sleigh by harnessing her to a metal trash can ballasted with heavy rocks. Back home next summer Jacqueline invested twenty dollars in an antiquated four-wheel buggy with a collapsible leather hood. Soon beautiful Danseuse, trailing a buggy loaded with kids, was gaily trotting into town on vital ice-cream-cone-buying errands.

Jacqueline with her mother's famous mare, Danseuse. Danseuse, a show ring champion, was also a beloved pet. She was a member of the family for twenty years.

When Donny died, Jacqueline created a photographic history of her life, linking the snapshots together with touching commentary: "Danseuse was a family horse and every child had a ride on her. She was such a lady. Her coat glinted in the sun when she was brushed and shining. She knew how lovely she was and flicked her tiny feet out in front of her as she trotted. There was a soft, pink spot at the end of her nose and she would snuffle softly when she knew you had an apple for her."

When Donny died, Jacqueline knew that a part of her youth went with her.

When Jacqueline was old enough to hold a pencil or crayon she began to write stories and poems and to illustrate them with drawings which were, even in the beginning, remarkably imaginative. Many of her baby "writings" were lost, of course, but gradually Janet, like many another loving mother, started to save the verses and stories penned in a firm ornamental writing and bordered with drawings. The stories were written on sheets of thick, white note paper and the succeeding pages tied together with bits of ribbon or brightly colored string.

Her first poem, written when she was eight, runs like this:

CHRISTMAS

Christmas is coming
Santa Claus is near
Reindeer hooves will soon be drumming
On the roof tops loud and clear
The shops are filled with people
Snow is coming down
And everyone is merry
In such a busy town.

Jacqueline was encouraged by Grampy Jack, her Bouvier grandfather, who composed the first of many successive birthday poems to his granddaughter when she was one. They were sentimental poems, replete with classical allusions yet meticulously correct in rhyme and meter. When his granddaughter reached fourteen, he wrote:

TO THE YOUTHFUL ARTEMIS

Diana, Mistress of the Chase,
And of all sylvan arts the Queen
Performing with supremest grace,
The sports on which the healthful lean.

Favorites sometimes caught her eye,
and 'Tis to them her skill she lent;
All in the days that have gone bye;
Of Ancient Times, how long since spent.

But strange, sweet maiden, to relate
She has since crowned a modern Queen,
Nor did her ART one jot abate,
When 'twas bestowed on Jacqueline.

     Congratulations, Gramps.

Later, when Jacqueline sent him for criticism her more ambitious poetic efforts, Grampy Jack's replies were, as always, wonderfully amusing. When she was twelve, he wrote:

My dear Jacqueline:
Holy Writ informs us that it was a futile labor to paint the lily white, and it is equally fatuous for me to attempt the perfecting of the perfect, in any suggested emendations to your delightful lines.
On the other hand, I am a bold technician, and have been impelled to suggest a few inconsequential verbal

Poem was written when Jacqueline was fourteen and later revised. She omitted the fourth stanza and added:

> "The tangy taste of apples,
> The snowy mist at morn,
> The wanderlust inside you when
> You hear the huntsman's horn.
> Nostalgia—that's the autumn.
> Dreaming through September.
> Just a million things I
> Always will remember."

alterations that perhaps do not add a d—n to your verses, but may, never-the-less tend to bring them within some textbook of rules of scansion. Your idea is extremely clever, and you have developed it admirably.

       Affectionately,
          GRAMPS

A year or so later Grampy Jack encouraged her to keep up their correspondence. The first paragraph of a long letter ran:

My dear Jackie:

No assurance was more gratefully received than was the expression of your resolution that you are going to write me "lots now." It is an engaging promise, similar, I think to those fine spiritual resolutions we make after receiving Communion, but, unhappily, our zeal, as in the case of the Spiritual Feast, later "spindles off into a sheaf of twigs." However, I am eager to establish an unbroken correspondence such, for example, as is reputed to have existed between Horace Walpole and Lord Chesterfield....

Her first stories were mostly delightful tales about various family animals. There was the "Adventures of George Woofty, Esq." a pet terrier—his imaginary romance with Caprice, a sleek, dark bouvier-des-Flandres lady dog whom Jacqueline's father had given his daughters because of the similarity of names. There was the "Life of Gen. de Gaulle," an amusing biography of a blasé black poodle. There were birthday poems to her mother and father and for family anniversaries of all kinds.

As she grew older Jacqueline's sense of fun heightened, her imagination sharpened, and she developed a satiric twist, ineffably touched with sweetness. Her cleverest, perhaps, in this vein was a tongue-in-cheek string of

Driving her piebald pony, Dancestep, Jacqueline rode in a pony cart in the costume parade for East Hampton's tercentenary celebration. (BERT & RICHARD MORGAN)

decade-in-the-future predictions for each member of the family. Each was intimate, gaggy. For herself she foresaw a future as the circus queen who, though admired by the world's biggies, married "the man on the flying trapeze."

Her skill as an artist grew, too. She went through a clever, single-line drawing phase which smacked of Steinberg; a wonderfully elaborate period when she illustrated a poem incidental to a gay, post-debutante trip to Europe with beautifully drawn, excitingly colored, and deliciously imaginative pictures.

Her teachers in school and later in college appreciated and encouraged both these talents. One, a favorite English professor, commented to a member of the family shortly after President Kennedy's election: "I always knew that Jacqueline would make a name for herself someday. But I really thought it would be by writing a book."

"She was someone you'd never forget," said Marion Eaton, art teacher at Miss Chapin's School, "she was very lively and full of mischief. She had great green eyes and wonderful hair."

Mary Platt, Jacqueline's "Room" teacher when she was ten, remembered, "She was one of the most beautiful children I ever saw. I glimpsed her when she was acting in a children's play, the year before she was in my class. I asked who she was. I don't remember her being especially good at drawing or painting. In every art class there are just a few who stand out—and even fewer who are completely incapable. I'd have remembered if she had been especially talented—or very bad. Jacqueline was interesting," she concluded, "and very mischievous."

Miss Affleck, another "Room" teacher, who had not seen Jacqueline for over twenty years, remembered her well. "She was a darling child," Miss Affleck enthused. "She was the prettiest little girl, very clever, very artistic, and full of the devil. She was efficient and finished her work on time and then had nothing to do until her classmates finished theirs."

"I was rather a tomboy," Jacqueline has often said. And summers in East Hampton, when all the Bouvier cousins were growing up together, she did her level best to keep up with the boys. There was a squad of Bouviers then, rather like the regiment of younger-generation Kennedys in Hyannis Port today. Her favorite contemporary was "Scotty" Scott (Henry Clarkson Scott) son of one of her twin aunts. She loved him "most" because he was an extremely bad boy. She was delighted when he permitted her to climb trees with him, or, on awesome occasions, pledged loyalty in blood-brother oaths. She "worshiped" her godfather, Michel Bouvier, who was a mere nine years her senior, because he treated her like an adult, and in him she imagined the big brother for whom she longed. "Miche" was always doing glamorous things, like going dancing and taking out girls. Because his father had died, he spent many summers at Lasata. Today they are still close and she is the godmother of his second son, who is named John Vernou Bouvier IV.

To balance her tomboyishness with ladylike activity, she attended two dancing classes each week. Miss Hubbell, who staged her fashionable sessions in the Colony Club, taught little girls—and little boys—modern ballroom dancing. The small boys wore Eton jackets or neat blue suits, the young ladies their very best party dresses. White gloves were musts for both. On these spit-and-polish occasions Jacqueline loosed her sensible braids into a cloud of shining black hair, and without demur put on her most feminine frock.

Jacqueline Bouvier and her sister Lee taken on a summer's day in East Hampton, where all the Bouviers gathered. "There was a squad of Bouviers rather like the regiment of younger Kennedys at Hyannis Port, Cape Cod, today." (IRVING CANTOR)

She enjoyed far more Miss O'Neill's ballet classes. For girls only, the lessons were strictly no-nonsense affairs at which the neophytes wore leotards and the basic movements of classical ballet were taught. Jacqueline proved so talented that at the spring recital, to which parents were invited, she tiptoed a solo number of Debussy's "Golliwog's Cakewalk."

When she was still very young Jacqueline commenced collecting a little library of her own, all on the ballet. She knew she could never be a ballet dancer but she did think, for a bit, that she might be part of the show, by designing ballet and theatrical costumes. She steeped herself in romantic literature, reading *Gone with the Wind* three times when she was eleven, and as she edged into her teens Lord Byron became a beloved companion. She read and reread his poems and lived his life through the pages of André Maurois's biography.

Jacqueline's sister, Caroline Lee Bouvier, is temperamentally totally different. Jacqueline did everything vehemently. When she stamped a letter, for instance, she pounded the stamp in place with her fist. When she started to read one book of an author, she continued on voraciously, through every volume he had written. Lee tended to be practical and had a built-in, soothing social instinct. Jacqueline was, in every way, a quick thing. Quick to anger, she never bore a grudge. Lee, so much younger, was like a chubby, bumbling puppy, always eager to please. Her older sister, at times, was very impatient with her.

Whenever little Jacqueline tossed a tantrum within earshot of her paternal grandmother, the adoring Mrs. Bouvier would alibi her with an indulgent: "Why that's only Jackie's French temperament showing!" Jacqueline's French temperament, however, is several generations removed from France for the first Bouvier to reach America, a French soldier, was present at the Yorktown Surrender in 1781. Nevertheless, within hours of her husband's election, the former Jacqueline Bouvier received cables from the mayors of half a dozen French towns, each proudly emphasizing that the Bouvier family had stemmed from his community. This enthusiastic confusion was understandable since in the 1770s no fewer than twenty-four adventurous Bouviers are recorded as having followed General Lafayette across the Atlantic to fight for American freedom. The French Ministry of Foreign Affairs listed their names in *Les Combattants Français de la Guerre Americaine 1778–1783*, a pamphlet which the United States Senate later republished. But Jacqueline's great-great-great-grandfather escaped official cataloguing because the roster of his regiment was lost.

His name was André Eustache Bouvier and his family was an "ancient house of Fontaine near Grenoble" which traced its line back to the early fifteenth century. Eustache was born in 1758 in Grenoble, a city which later strongly supported the young American colonies in their struggle for freedom. He enlisted in the Grenoble Artillery Regiment, led by a Captain Savournin, and was twenty-two when his unit, one of four regiments under General Rochambeau's command, participated in the British surrender at Yorktown, which climaxed the War of American Independence.

In 1783 Eustache went home to France and six years later, at thirty-one, married Therese Mercier in Pont St. Esprit. Eustache never returned to America. But he must have loved the young country for which he had fought and transferred this affection to his son, Michel, who became the first Bouvier to settle permanently in the new world. When still a teen-ager he imitated his father's military inclination and left Pont St. Esprit to serve with Napoleon. Somewhere during the campaigns, Michel made an impression on Joseph Bonaparte, King of Spain, and brother to Napoleon. Shortly before Napoleon's final defeat Joseph abdicated, sailed for the United States, and settled down to comfortable everyday life in Bordentown, New Jersey. Soon afterwards Michel followed to nearby Philadelphia. It was 1815, he was twenty-three, and the enterprising youth found in the former monarch a generous patron and kind friend.

Michel married Louise Vernou, daughter of a Frenchman of noble family who had fled to Philadelphia during the French Revolution. As a manufacturer of veneer and an importer of Italian marble and the costly woods used in cabinet work, he accumulated what was then reckoned a "palatial fortune." When Michel died at the ripe age of eighty-four, a laudatory obituary reported he had "commenced business with the grand capital of integrity, industry, economy, enterprise and perserverence" and though "he loved the paths of commerce and social companionship—with him they were all connected with the home." Thirteen years after his death, Philadelphia named a Bouvier Street in his honor.

Of the ten surviving Bouvier children, a daughter, Emma, married Francis A. Drexel whose brother was powerful head of the Drexel banking firm and senior partner of the elder J. Pierpont Morgan.

Another of Michel and Louise's successful children, the first John Vernou Bouvier, was Jacqueline's great-grandfather. He fitted into the Bouvier pattern by soldiering in his teens, becoming a business success in his early twenties, marrying happily, and living well over eighty years. At eighteen he enlisted as a private in the Second Pennsylvania Infantry of the Northern Forces. The youngster was soon detailed as aide-de-camp to General Patrick, commander of the Second Brigade, Department of the Rappahannock. Some months later he was taken prisoner when seriously wounded fighting at Groveton, Virginia. Bouvier family legend has it that the young officer, left for dead on the battlefield, was saved when an old colored slave heard his moans. Whether the story is apochryphal or not, John Vernou Bouvier was proud of his terrible wound and would occasionally permit his grandchildren, among them Jacqueline's father, the treasured privilege of viewing the scar which zigzagged across his chest!

This picturesque wound almost prevented John Vernou Bouvier's marriage, at twenty-one, to Caroline Ewing. She was the beautiful daughter of Robert Ewing of Philadelphia and of Caroline Maslin, namesake of her native Caroline County in Maryland. (This is the origin of Caroline Kennedy's name!) Caroline's parents had two objections to the match. First, the young man's severe wound had destroyed a lung. This, they felt, might make Caroline a widow in short order. Second, Bouvier was a Roman Catholic. Happily, the presumably delicate bridegroom lived to a hearty eighty-three. The bride was converted to her husband's religion and the marriage spanned sixty-one rewarding years. Caroline spent all possible time in good works and after her husband made a fortune, she established the New York Foundling Hospital where unwanted children were accepted regardless of race, color or presumed creed. It was this admirable lady for whom both Mrs. Kennedy's sister and daughter were lovingly named.

Jacqueline Kennedy's energetic great-grandfather soon moved with his Caroline from Philadelphia to New York. In 1869 when he was twenty-six, he invested $5,000 in a New York Stock Exchange seat. When he retired in 1920, a wise and affluent seventy-nine, he sold this same membership for $115,000, then a record price. As the Bouviers were always a close-knit family, John Vernou Bouvier's younger brother Michel C. Bouvier, when a mere twenty-two, also bought a seat on the Stock Exchange. Four years later, during the Panic of 1873, when financial failures were so frequent that the New York Stock Exchange was closed to prevent further chaos, young Michel's business ability was held in such high esteem that the head of one of the foremost trust companies, trembling on the verge of folding, asked him to take over Commodore Cornelius Vanderbilt's multimillion dollar accounts. Since the Vanderbilt accounts were not legitimately related to trust company affairs, they were entitled to protection. The request was a tremendous compliment but nevertheless an equally tremendous responsibility.

Michel soon set up his own firm which became M. C. Bouvier & Company and in which both John Vernou Bouvier Jr. and John Vernou Bouvier III, Jacqueline's grandfather and father, were at one time partners. A bachelor, Michel was a popular figure in New York's social world. He resided with three spinster sisters, Zenaide, Alexine, and Mary, in a great house on West 46th Street, from which they refused to move though the once-fashionable neighborhood became completely taken over by office buildings. The trio of sisters, who lived to typically Bouvier advanced age, were extremely pious and maintained in their home a private chapel in which Mass was celebrated. They devoted much of their lives to hospital and charity work and when Miss Mary died at ninety-one, it was discovered that she was supporting more than fifty private pensioners. Michel survived his sisters, living through eighty-nine busy years. A member of the New York Stock

Exchange for over sixty-six years, he was known as the dean of the Wall Street brokers and business associates agreed that he typified "what was best, fair and true, intelligent and efficient in the Wall Street Broker."

When Jacqueline was old enough to be companionable with her grandfather, John Vernou Bouvier, Jr., he was over seventy. Extremely fastidious, he wore the high starched collar, pince-nez eyeglasses, formal suits and pointed waxed mustachios which even in the thirties were *de rigueur* for a gentleman of his age and position. To Jacqueline and her younger sister, Lee, he was Grampy Jack, an affectionate nickname which, to outsiders, seemed altogether unsuitable. He took great delight in this very special granddaughter and helped to develop her literary talents. They corresponded even though both were often in New York. While his courtly letters were studded with classical allusions and his loftily expressed advice was sensible, he never talked down to her and very early discovered in Jacqueline qualities of leadership which, by his high standards, he tried to guide into the right path.

This agreeable gentleman was the only child of Caroline and John Vernou Bouvier. He was an intellectual genius who entered Columbia University at sixteen and emerged four years later with a B.A. degree, a Phi Beta Kappa key, a prize for winning the Chanler Historical Essay and triple collegiate rewards as Honor Man, Valedictorian and Vice President of the Class of 1886. By the time he was twenty-two, he had earned a M.A. in Political Science, graduated from the Columbia Law School with a Litt.D and passed his New York State Bar Examinations. John Vernou Bouvier, Jr., specializing in corporation work, became one of New York's most brilliant trial lawyers. As change of pace, when he was well over sixty, he took a sedate flyer in the brokerage business by joining the firm of his uncle Michel Bouvier. He was a much quoted authority on both George Washington and the United States Constitution and in great demand as an after-dinner speaker on his favorite subjects. He would have gotten on admirably with his history-loving grandson-in-law, John F. Kennedy.

As they grew older, the two Bouvier sisters became very close. They saw a great deal of their parents who both made them feel securely loved. So when Janet and Jack Bouvier decided that their marriage had reached a state where it was wiser for them to live separately, the children's normal routine was not unduly upset. The girls and their mother moved from the Park Avenue duplex to a smaller apartment near Miss Chapin's School. The sisters spent every Sunday, half of every term-time school vacation, and six weeks in summer with their father.

The sisters idolized their father. He was so big, so handsome, so dashing, and he gave them so much fun. He liked horse shows, dog shows, and anything to do with animals, prize fights, dancing. At East Hampton he promoted weekend baseball teams, the Bouvier's Black Ducks against fisherman Kip Farrington's Mugwumps. He drove his car very fast and was always deeply suntanned and proud of dressing fastidiously. He was a stockbroker like his grandfather and great-uncle, but, being younger and less well established, suffered more from the up-and-down quirks of the New York Stock Exchange. He had an imaginative, mischievous side to his nature which made him the greatest companion to the young, and the little girls' friends simply ate him up.

He encouraged the girls to climb trees, learn to ride no-handed on a bicycle, and was the despair of their nurses because he let them eat sweets too soon before

Mrs. Kennedy's favorite photograph of her father, John Vernou Bouvier III, was made when she was six and winner, as usual, of a ribbon in a Long Island horse show. (IRA A. HILL)

dinner. He encouraged their incipient gourmet tastes by introducing them to pistachio ice cream, an edible they both still adore. Every year Jack Bouvier produced entry blanks for the Kentucky Colonel tobacco contest. The gambit was that whoever suggested just the right name would win a Kentucky yearling. Unfortunately, the Bouvier sisters never won. He was sympathetic, too, when, aged nine and six, they became dreadfully concerned with vivisection. He helped write out telegrams expressing their anguished disapproval with vivisection and dispatched them to the New York *Journal-American,* which was then headlining the anti-vivisectionist cause.

Sundays, when their father called for them, he would toot the secret Bouvier signal, a series of long and short notes, on his automobile horn. (Jacqueline whistled it to Caroline the other day and she was very much intrigued.) Off they would go. At first the smaller apartment had seemed too cramped to permit keeping a dog, and the children missed a pet. So their father arranged a "deal" with the proprietors of several pet shops. The three would pick out one of the stores, go inside, choose the dogs for whom they felt sorriest and then take them for a long run in Central Park. A deposit was made to cover possible loss and paid back when the refreshed canines returned.

Sometimes a number of little pals would be invited to lunch at Schrafft's, go to a movie, and polish off the afternoon with a sure-fire supper ruiner, a round of sundaes at the nearest drugstore. Occasionally the three would go up to Baker's Field at Columbia University, a spot usually deserted on winter Sundays, and play in the outdoor rowing seats set up for sculling practice. In the spring they might watch baseball tryouts at Baker's Field,

Mrs. John Vernou Bouvier III and her daughters were walking to a wedding when a photographer caught this picture. (BERT & RICHARD MORGAN)

or perhaps motor out to Belmont Park, where they would be introduced to top-flight jockeys in the paddock.

Jacqueline's most vivid memories spotlight trips downtown to lunch in Wall Street, passing by the Fulton Fish Market, and one red-letter day her father took her to the New York Stock Exchange gallery. There she looked down in wonder at the incredible maelstrom of shouting, jostling stockbrokers, which was so much part of her father's masculine world.

Jack Bouvier, who died in 1957, never remarried. He met his son-in-law before Jacqueline and Jack were married. They went out together to dinner that night and the two Jacks got along so famously that Jackie was completely left out of the conversation. They both had the same rather irreverent kind of humor and enjoyed talking about sports and politics.

After the Kennedys were married they lunched with him in Wall Street and the senior Jack showed the junior Jack around his special bailiwick, the New York Stock Exchange.

When Jack and Jacqueline owned Hickory Hill, a house just outside Washington, Jack Bouvier would weekend with them. Evenings, companionably, the Senator and his father-in-law would watch the big fights on TV.

Shortly before election, Senator and Mrs. Kennedy rode down Wall Street in the giant ticker-tape parade which traditionally winds through the financial district. Two millions, it was said, jammed the sidewalks to glimpse the presidential candidate and his wife perched on the back of their car. Police battled frantically to keep the cheering crowds from toppling the Kennedy automobile as it came to a halt in Wall Street.

Amidst the hubbub Jack Kennedy leaned over to Jacqueline. "Isn't it too bad that your father couldn't be

In World War I, John Vernou Bouvier III was a second lieutenant in the coast artillery. A Yale graduate, he became a member of the New York Stock Exchange in 1919.

with us in this car today?" he almost shouted. "He'd have really enjoyed seeing this."

It was one of the great moments of John Fitzgerald Kennedy's life and his wife, who had been thinking of her father as the car inched along, nodded. Her eyes were very bright.

Part Two

JACQUELINE BOUVIER was not quite fourteen when a new phase of her life commenced. Her mother remarried in June 1942, and the two sisters, Jacqueline and Lee, left New York to join their stepfather, Hugh D. Auchincloss. Their future home would be in winter dignified, Georgian-style Merrywood, set in woods high on the Virginia shore across the Potomac from Washington, and in summer Hammersmith Farm, a rambling, Victorian tea cozy of a house overlooking seventy-five acres of farmland fringing fashionable Newport.

Now the two girls would no longer be the only children in the family. Their stepfather had two sons and a daughter. The elder son, Hugh, Jr. (Yusha), a bit Jacqueline's senior, had always lived with his father. Soon, the younger son and daughter, Nini and Tommy, were to return home. Five years later, after Jacqueline's half-sister and brother had been born, there were seven young people of varying ages and temperaments, who called Merrywood and Hammersmith Farm home.

Janet took care of them all. "Aunt Janet was really my mother," said one of her stepchildren gratefully, "she did as much for us as she did for her own children."

Though Janet Lee Bouvier was an Episcopalian and hence not barred by religious conviction, a second marriage had been a difficult decision. When she and Jack Bouvier separated, she determined to devote her life to raising their daughters. During her years alone she never left the small girls for even a weekend. But she was a beautiful young woman and, naturally, a magnet to men.

The 1945 Christmas greetings from Hugh and Janet Auchincloss pictures them, seated with baby Janet Jennings. Jacqueline at top, with Yusha (Hugh D. Auchincloss, Jr.). Middle Row: Nina and Thomas Auchincloss and Lee Bouvier.

Hugh Dudley Auchincloss possessed the kindly qualities Janet admired. He was steadfast and unshakably serene in any crisis. He was generous and equipped with a nice, slow-starting sense of humor. In fact, he was just what Jacqueline often said he was, "a wonderful stepfather."

His Auchincloss ancestors, two canny brothers from Glasgow, arrived to make their fortunes in America during the early nineteenth century. Hugh, like his father, was born in Newport. A graduate of Yale and Columbia Law School, he had left New York law practice in the early '30s, worked a Government stint, mostly at drafting diplomatic documents, and after a wartime naval assignment set up a Washington stock-brokerage firm. Like almost everyone who has enjoyed living in the capital, he was reluctant to leave.

The two Auchincloss places made a happy background for the seven children. Merrywood is a generous house containing a string of bedrooms, and the forty-six acres of woodsy grounds are studded with conveniences handy to the active young—a swimming pool, an enclosed badminton court, and a small stable where ponies and Janet's mare, Danseuse, were bedded cozily.

(Jacqueline and Jack Kennedy spent the first summer of their marriage at Merrywood. Here Jacqueline gave her initial party as a senator's wife, celebrating Pat Kennedy's marriage to Peter Lawford, the motion-picture star. Congress was still in session and that sultry July night guests, arriving late from work at the Capitol, swam before and after dinner, between times sitting at small, gaily decorated tables around the lighted pool. The only flaw in Jacqueline's perfect fun evening was her husband's health. The Senator, soon to undergo a serious corrective operation for war injury, was on crutches and could neither dance nor swim.)

Hammersmith Farm was part of Hugh Auchincloss' Rhode Island heritage. The property once covered over a thousand acres and originally belonged to William Brenton, the first Royal Surveyor, who hailed from Hammersmith, in England. The house was built in 1888 by an uncle and acquired by Hugh's parents shortly before his birth. On the farm were stables for work horses and a few pet sheep and goats, barns for bulls and the proprietor's favored Guernsey cows. Once corn had been planted, hay harvested. Until recently, when upkeep became too difficult, there had been elaborate rose beds, sunken and rock gardens which the younger children were detailed to weed.

Inside, the house was sunny, drafty, filled with comfortable, old-fashioned furniture. (Hammersmith Farm was extensively modernized two years ago.) There were numberless animal heads ornamenting the walls. In the Deck Room, focal point of the main floor, a stuffed pelican, in realistically awkward flight, still hangs from the ceiling. In the downstairs rooms and long halls, the walls were white, the carpets red. To round out this color scheme, Jacqueline decreed that all family dogs should be black. They were. There was Jacqueline's bouvier des Flandres, Caprice; Lee's poodle, General de Gaulle; and later Janet's Scotty, Corkscrew; and Nini Auchincloss' black cocker, Puddles.

The children all slept on the third floor. Jacqueline's bower had yellow wallpaper topped with a broad band of flowers bordering the white ceiling. The simple wooden furniture was painted white, and the headboard of the bed inset with a caned panel. There was a small shelf for her girlhood collection of china animals. Jacqueline slept in this room when she was "selected" as New York's most glamorous debutante. She left it as a bride. Now-

In a sophisticated mood, Jacqueline was snapped against a canvas-covered tennis-court wall at Newport. (LLOYD S. PAULEY)

adays when she visits her family alone, she returns to her old, familiar room.

She loved both Merrywood and Hammersmith Farm. During the winter she spent at the Sorbonne she wrote her step-brother, Yusha: "I always love it so at Merrywood—so peaceful—with the river and the dogs—and listening to the Victrola. I will never know which I love best—Hammersmith with its green fields and summer winds—or Merrywood in the snow—with the river and those great steep hills. I love them both—whichever I'm at—just as passionately as I loved the one I left behind."

A few summers later when she was motoring through Italy, Jacqueline wrote her stepfather: "I began to feel terribly homesick as I was driving—just like a dream—I started thinking of things like the path leading to the stable at Merrywood with the stones slipping as you ran up it—and Hammersmith with the foghorns blowing at night—all the places and feelings and happiness that bind you to a family you love—something that you take with you no matter how far you go."

(When her mother and step-father had been married ten years Jacqueline, then twenty-three, wrote a series of brief poems each humorously spotlighting an "important" event made possible only by Janet and Hugh's marriage. Her charming introduction read: "It seems so hard to believe that you've been married ten years. I think they must have been the very best decade of your lives. At the start, in 1942, we all had other lives and we were seven people thrown together, so many little separate units that could have stayed that way. Now we are nine —and what you've given us and what we've shared has bound us all to each other for the rest of our lives."

Less mischievous than in her days at Miss Chapin's School Jacqueline really enjoyed studying during a two-year span at Holton-Arms, a private Washington day school. She discovered that her stepfather's advice was true. "Always take the course given by the best teacher," Uncle Hugh had said, "even if you're not interested in the subject." Her most inspiring teacher was Miss Helen Shearman, who later was to chaperon Jacqueline and three friends on their first trip to Europe. Miss Shearman taught Latin. She demanded a great deal from her pupils and sometimes Jacqueline thought Miss Shearman too exigent. "But she was right. We were all lazy teen-agers," Jacqueline emphasized years afterwards. "Everything she taught me stuck and, though I hated to admit it, I adored Latin."

While Jacqueline was learning to like a dead language she was also learning a new live language. She had had French lessons since she was a small child and now, at Holton-Arms, Spanish was added to the curriculum. To her intense pleasure, one of the first words she picked up was *caramba*, a Spanish swear word.

She confided this piquant fact immediately in a letter to Grampy Jack. John Vernou Bouvier, Jr. answered in his usual dressy phrases:

> Exactly why your Spanish teacher should instruct you how to swear in that tongue I am a little perplexed to understand. *Caramba* is agreeable to the ear and if my knowledge is correct means nothing more than an innocuous "damn it," but if, at the time you are expressing it, you stamp your foot impatiently, pirouette slightly, throw your arms upward and heave your bosom, the whole makes for an impressive ensemble and lends a certain amount of weight and dignity to the word which otherwise would be practically meaningless. But I see no particular virtue in cultivating *caramba*, however adorned.

Like many other well-placed Washington girls, Jacqueline attended Miss Shippen's dancing classes. During the vacations there were real dances given to which boys were invited. At the Christmas party Jacqueline wore her first grown-up evening dress, which her mother bought. It was blue taffeta, full-skirted, puff-sleeved. Gold kid slippers completed the costume and, as Jacqueline's feet had grown faster than the rest of her, she was self-conscious about them. She caricatured her pretty getup later in one of her illustrated rhymes. The caption read: "Jacqueline's first evening dress. This was lovely blue taffeta and I had a pair of gold track shoes and a really chic feather cut."

When Jacqueline was fifteen she went off to Miss Porter's School at Farmington, Connecticut. A very old school, crammed with New England atmosphere, it was founded in 1843 by Miss Porter, a remarkably advanced feminine educator, daughter of a Congregational minister and sister of Noah Porter who became president of Yale University.

Miss Porter started with ten or a dozen girls, housing them in a small local hotel originally built for canal passengers. She had bought it at a bargain when railroads put the waterway out of business. As the school expanded Miss Porter purchased neighboring houses, big, white-clapboarded, old-fashioned, which ranged along Farmington's main street. By Civil War time Miss Porter's seminary was famed throughout the country. Now there are around an hundred and ninety pupils, many of them daughters, granddaughters and even great-granddaughters of former students.

Today the Farmington girls live very much as did Miss Porter's first dozen: two to a large, cheerily wallpapered room, furnished with twin mahogany beds, desks, and easy chairs. Each of the seven dormitory houses has a housemother, an understanding person who functions as chaperon, confidante, and general comforter.

(Jacqueline, who sometimes doubted she'd ever marry, once wrote to a Farmington friend: "I just know no one will ever marry me and I'll end up as a house mother at Farmington.")

The girls take turns waiting on table and are sometimes invited to after-dinner coffee by teachers. Greatest thrills, of course, happen on weekends. Then visiting parents may treat their daughters and best friends to steak luncheons and dinners at the Elm Tree Inn in Farmington. On Saturdays older girls are permitted "callers." Callers—male, naturally—wend their way to Farmington from Yale, Harvard, and other institutions of higher learning. They arrive punctually at two P.M. They leave with equal punctuality after tea at the headmaster's house.

Farmington was a minor paradise for Jacqueline. She liked her studies. She liked having Danseuse in the school stable. She liked her roommate—first Sue Norton, then Nancy Tuckerman, whose parents were family friends. It was pleasant, too, to take friends to the Wilmarth Lewises for especially scrumptious chocolate cake and a peek at their fascinating library. "Lefty" Lewis a famous scholar and ultimate expert on Blake and Walpole, was married to a sister of Uncle Hugh's. The Lewises fanned Jacqueline's interest in literature and each Christmas gave her some rare book, often on art.

Today when anyone is baffled as to what to give Jacqueline for Christmas, the answer is an art book, with "master drawings" her particular delight. (Jacqueline feels guilty at suggesting such a gift since these volumes are very costly. But to guide relatives and close friends at holiday time, she has left a list of books she'd like to own at a bookstore near her former house in Georgetown.)

As usual, she did very well in her studies at Farmington. Her grades averaged around A minus. Her mother, though, became very much annoyed with Ward L. Johnson, the headmaster, when he sent her Jacqueline's reports. For, no matter how high her marks, Mr. Johnson would invariably comment, "Jacqueline could do better," or "Jacqueline is not making her best effort." Jacqueline, in turn, when writing home used to dot her letters with irreverently comic sketches of the headmaster. In retrospect, Mr. Johnson, who did not teach, loomed large in her life as a moral force comparable only to Miss Ethel Stringfellow of Miss Chapin's School because of his "great understanding."

There were three courses at Miss Porter's in which Jacqueline delighted. Her favorite was History of Art, given by Miss Sarah McLennen, a strict, brilliant teacher. Runners-up were Miss Watson's English and Miss Coman's Special Literature. All three instructors were hard taskmasters. "You had to work to win their approval," said Jacqueline, "and when you did it meant something!" Miss Watson gave her an appreciation of good writing and helped her through drilling in grammar and vocabulary study. Miss Coman, more passionate and imaginative, stirred her profound interest in poetry and early English literature.

During her first term at Miss Porter's wise Grampy Jack Bouvier wrote his much-loved granddaughter a letter which was, in a way, a code of behavior.

Dear Jacqueline:

The capacity to adapt oneself to his or her environment not only marks evolutionary progress, but discloses a practical philosophy which is more wise to cultivate.

With you, happily, this process of adaption has not

been in the remotest degree difficult. You enjoy Farmington and all the things it has to offer, the most important among which is the adequate preparation for future feats of work and responsibility. . . . I discern in you more than passing evidence of leadership, but before leading others we must guide and direct ourselves. This is the true way of usefulness in life. . . . You will observe that those who are useful are the best contributors to the correct leading of life and in the last analysis are the most efficient and most contented members of all God's creatures. But don't be pretentious or labor under false impression of indispensability. To do so spells the prig, either male or female. . .

Affectionately,
GRANDFATHER

Perhaps Grampy Jack's admonitions account in part for his granddaughter's very genuine modesty. But, besides Jacqueline's scholastic effort, her "preparation for future feats of work and responsibility" included considerable deviltry. One mid-term when everyone was bored Jacqueline, whose turn it was to wait on the table, accepting a dare, artfully dropped chocolate pie upside down in a teacher's lap. Amidst a gale of giggles, she was sent from the dining room. Her most spectacular stunt, repeated regularly, was swiping cookies—freshly baked ones. The cookies were baked on the weekend and cached safely in the kitchen. It was difficult for an unauthorized person to penetrate this sanctum. Nevertheless, Jacqueline often managed to infiltrate after the Sunday evening lecture and make off with enough cookies to last "Tucky" and herself through the week. This derring-do was locally much admired.

That winter Jacqueline managed to have Miss Porter's old sleigh, which had been stored for half a century, reactivated for Donny. She spent so much time training Donny to pull it and generally caring for the mare that she took little part in athletics. But she worked like a beaver on anything literary. She was a board member of *The Salamagundy*, the school newspaper, and contributed both poems and cartoons. She was a moving spirit among The Players, a theatrical group which produced a Christmas tableau and two full-length plays each year. A master vividly recalls her acting the leading role in a "German," an impromptu pantomime which is a specialty at Miss Porter's. "Her interpretive acting, all in pantomime, was remarkable." Then he added: "Jacqueline was very bright and had such lovely manners." One of her roommates remembered: "She could learn anything in a snap. At study hall she'd finish first of anyone—then she'd spend the rest of her time sketching—and writing poems."

(Jacqueline's practice in pantomiming paid off. A few years ago when the Kennedys still had a bit of leisure, one of their favorite after-dinner party sports was "The Game," in which two opposing teams, struggling against time, act out a given word, syllable by syllable. The team guessing the word quickest wins. All Kennedys are as expert at "The Game" as they are at touch football—and as hard to beat. Jacqueline is the most skilled pantomimer of all.)

Among her happiest Farmington memories were the weekends her father visited. John Vernou Bouvier III came to see his daughter act, to partner her in daughter-father tennis tournaments, to watch her carry off trophies at local horse shows on Danseuse. "All my Farmington friends loved daddy," Jacqueline recalls. "He'd take batches of us out to luncheon at the Elm Tree Inn. Everybody ordered steaks and two desserts. We must have eaten him broke."

When she graduated from Miss Porter's, Jacqueline was pinpointed in the class yearbook's gaggy profile.

JACQUELINE LEE BOUVIER
"MERRYWOOD"
MC LEAN, VIRGINIA
"Jackie"

Favorite Song: Lime House Blues
Always Saying: "Play a Rhumba next"
Most Known For: Wit
Aversion: People who ask if her horse is still alive
Where Found: Laughing with Tucky
Ambition: Not to be a housewife

Jacqueline's ambition was easily achieved.

When she was fifteen her half-sister, Janet Jennings Auchincloss, was born. Jacqueline commemorated this event by dedicating a gay birthday poem to her mother, entitled "Janet Jennings—Her Life and Times." The jingly poem, written in the tempo of "The Midnight Ride of Paul Revere," amusingly parallels the excitement when her own little son was born this past Thanksgiving.

"Listen, my children, and you shall hear," the rhyme commences, "of a thing that delighted the hemisphere. It was nineteen hundred and forty-five when Janet Jennings became alive. She made all the headlines far and near and became the Baby of the Year! Crowds to do her homage came, bringing priceless gifts and rare. The flower shops all had a boom and Western Union tore its hair."

Then, skipping a few stanzas, Jacqueline continues her

fun: "Into my crystal ball I gaze and predict a future that will amaze." The predicted future foresaw Janet Jennings entering politics at twenty-one. Then, "First woman President you'll be, I trow." The finale is several verses later: "You'll live a rich, full life all right. The oppressed you'll always free 'em and when dead you'll have a statue in Tussaud's Wax Museum!"

(A wax model of Jacqueline's husband joined other American presidents and statesmen in Madame Tussaud's Museum in London on Inauguration Day.)

Today Janet Jennings Auchincloss is sixteen and enjoying her second year at Miss Porter's School. She is full of bounce, but so far shows little indication of fulfilling her sister's prophecy of becoming political-minded.

Jamie Auchincloss, youngest of the family, was born a few months before Jacqueline was graduated from Farmington. He is, undoubtedly, one of the very few young men who at the age of five months, shared a debutante party with an older sister. It was a Tea, a reception with dancing, at Hammersmith Farm in Newport.

Jamie had been christened that same afternoon at Trinity Church, with the Dean of the Virginia Theological Seminary officiating. Engraved invitations to the debut-reception afterward had gone out in the name of his parents, Mr. and Mrs. Hugh Dudley Auchincloss and the legend included: "To meet Miss Jacqueline Lee Bouvier and Master James Lee Auchincloss."

Jamie, endowed with curly hair and regular features, despite being somewhat hampered by long christening robes, maintained such poise that a knowledgeable dowager declared he looked "just like a senator." And the very next day after the christening cards had been mailed Jamie received his first social invitation. An eager

Jacqueline, photographed at Hammersmith Farm, Newport, before her "coming-out" dance. To the right of the fireplace is a Charles II high chair given to her half-brother, James Lee Auchincloss, by a godfather. Earlier that same summer Jacqueline and five-month-old "Jamie" shared honors at an afternoon Tea which jointly celebrated her debut and his christening. (ROBERT MESERVEY)

hostess, constantly alert for extra dancing men, bid Mr. James Lee Auchincloss to a dinner dance.

The nearby Providence *Journal* recorded the twin event:

Miss Jacqueline Bouvier, debutante daughter of Mrs. Hugh Auchincloss made her official bow to the social world yesterday when she was presented at an afternoon reception at the Auchincloss estate, Hammersmith Farm, with about three hundred persons in attendance. Miss Bouvier, who had been deluged with floral gifts during the day, received with Mr. Auchincloss and her mother. During the reception Mr. and Mrs. Auchincloss were being congratulated on the christening of their son, James L. Auchincloss.

(Jacqueline thinks her Tea with Jamie was "nice" and the way all coming-out parties should be—teas instead of expensive dances.)

At the Tea Jacqueline "met" her mother's friends, though of course, she had known most of them for years. Later that summer she was to share honors again, this time with Rose Grosvenor, a debutante daughter of the Theodore Grosvenors, at a dance. The party, mostly for the young, climaxed Tennis Week and was given at the Clambake Club, one of Newport's most cherished old institutions. Its completely masculine membership stages super-de luxe stag clambakes on the Fourth of July and Labor Day. Between holidays members relax, fish, and in autumn, when bathers have left the adjoining beaches, shoot clay pigeons. Ladies may be invited to share gargantuan meals of bean soup, clam chowder, broiled lobster and deep-dish apple pie, prepared by boss-chef Ruby, a Clambake Club factotem for thirty years.

The rustic club building perches atop rocks which jut

"Being nervous before," Jacqueline wrote under this photograph. She and Rose Grosvenor, left, anticipate their joint coming-out dance at the Clambake Club in Newport. (ROBERT MESERVEY)

into the ocean and, on a summer night, is a heavenly place.

This special evening the pine-paneled rooms were decorated with flowers cut from the Auchincloss and Grosvenor gardens and the terrace was necklaced with blue lights.

As they stood in the receiving line together, Rosie Grosvenor, blond, peachy, dimpled, made a fine foil for tanned, glowing Jacqueline. Jacqueline carried a nosegay of bouvardia and sweetheart roses. Newspapers described her dress as "a lovely white tulle gown with an off-the-shoulder neckline and bouffant skirt." Jacqueline, never a spender, had bought the frock off a New York department store rack. It had cost fifty-nine dollars. That spring and summer, after Jamie's birth, their mother had been slow to recover. She wasn't strong enough to shop and Jacqueline had been told to buy herself a coming-out dress, the most glamorous one possible. The simple gown was lovely but Janet, so proud of her daughter and wanting her to have the most ravishing of all creations, couldn't help being a bit disappointed.

The sartorial sensation that evening, however, was not made by debutante, matron, or dowager. Instead it was made by a kid sister, allowed after dinner to join the fun. This baby vamp, of course, was Lee Bouvier. A suitable juvenile frock had been selected for fourteen-year-old Lee. But she had other ideas and, by wiles never discovered, coaxed the local seamstress to run up a design of her own. It was strapless pink satin, sprinkled generously with rhinestones and sirenishly accessorized with elbow-length black satin mitts, fingerless, but tethered by a pointed strap over the middle finger. The stag line made a beeline for curvaceous, flirty Lee.

Later Jacqueline occasionally borrowed Lee's siren

suit and claims she was wearing it when Cholly Knickerbocker decided to nominate her as the year's Number One Debutante. The Hearst columnist, whose real name is Igor Cassini, wrote as follows:

> America is a country of traditions. Every four years we elect a President, every two years our congressmen. And every year a new Queen of Debutantes is crowned... Queen Deb of the Year is Jacqueline Bouvier, a regal brunette who has classic features and the daintiness of Dresden porcelain. She has poise, is soft-spoken and intelligent, everything the leading debutante should be. Her background is strictly "Old Guard."...Jacqueline is now studying at Vassar. You don't have to read a batch of press clippings to be aware of her qualities.

As result of this puff, Jacqueline was badgered by unwanted attention. It didn't disturb her too much. A New York columnist commented: "Jacqueline Bouvier, Queen Deb of the Year is being beseiged with offers of all sorts and demands for interviews and pictures—but her conservative family is shying away from all publicity." Said another news scribe slangily, but admiringly: "Jacqueline Bouvier's poise! What a gal! She's the beautiful daughter of Mrs. Hugh Auchincloss. Blessed with the looks of a fairy-tale princess, Jacqueline doesn't know the meaning of the word snob!"

After all the fun, all the beaux, all the summer parties, Jacqueline left Hammersmith Farm for college. She had passed her college-aptitude tests in the ninety percentile rating, the top-bracket group, achieved only by a very small percentage of students, and was offered admission to several colleges. She chose Vassar because so many of her friends were going there. She was to stay two years.

Masculine "callers" flocked to Vassar to see this authentic Glamour Girl. Weekends when she was permitted to leave Poughkeepsie she hurried to Yale, to Harvard, to New York to see her father or back home to Merrywood. She developed so many "admirers" that her father worried about losing her to one of them.

"I suppose it won't be long until I lose you to some funny-looking 'gink,'" he wrote, "who you think is wonderful because he is so romantic-looking in the evening and wears his mother's pearl earrings for dress-shirt buttons, because he loves her so.... However, perhaps you'll use your head and wait until you are at least twenty-one."

Contemporaries who had known Jacqueline a long time sensed that she was in a transient mood at Vassar. A childhood friend and college classmate interpreted her mood: Jacqueline was evolving, her personality was flowering. While so many of her age were static, set in their ways, Jacqueline constantly was discovering new interests. Her imagination was wonderfully offbeat. She never talked for talking's sake. And though she made friends easily, she was reserved without being cold and there were few who really knew her well.

Looking back, Jacqueline wishes she had gone away less or had fewer callers to absorb her time. Then she could have taken more advantage of Vassar's many opportunities.

Despite these extracurricular activities, Jacqueline maintained astonishingly high grades. Two courses were to give her the greatest intellectual pleasure. The first was History of Religion, taught by Miss Lovell, one of Vassar's outstanding professors. Jacqueline "loved" the course because of Miss Lovell's fascinating presentation of an unexpectedly dramatic subject.

Miss Helen Sandison's lectures on Shakespeare were

While Jacqueline was still a preschooler, teen-age Jack Kennedy was at Choate, and later was to go to Harvard and the London School of Economics. (BERT & RICHARD MORGAN)

"the greatest course I have ever had." Jacqueline found her "the most inspired teacher" and the one, in the eager student's experience, who "loved her subject most." Miss Sandison is responsible for her pupil's great passion for Shakespeare. She found her favorite poetry in Shakespeare's *Antony and Cleopatra* and at one time knew all its great passages by heart. Among these exquisite words Jacqueline discovered a single line which she ardently feels applies perfectly to her husband: "His delights were dolphin-like. He showed his back above the element he lived in."

"All my greatest interests—in literature and art, Shakespeare and poetry—were formed because I was fortunate enough to find superb teachers in these fields," Jacqueline Bouvier concluded.

She fell irrevocably in love with Europe on her first trip. The summer after her freshman year at Vassar Jacqueline, with three friends, made the Grand Tour, chaperoned by Miss Helen Shearman, the congenial Holton-Arms teacher. Two of her companions, Helen and Judy Bowdoin, were stepdaughters of Edward F. Foley, Jr., then Under Secretary of the Treasury. The fourth member of the group was Julia Bissell, of Wilmington. Months in advance, Under Secretary Foley arranged to have the girls and their chaperone invited to a Royal Garden Party at Buckingham Palace. So the quartet set sail on the *Queen Mary*, handsomely equipped by their mothers with the requisite dressy afternoon gowns, cartwheel straw hats, and two (in case one was mislaid) pairs of elbow-length white gloves.

The Garden Party was a mob scene. It poured rain and everyone had to jam somewhat stickily together under the refreshment marquees. Though the girls were not formally presented to King George VI and Queen

Elizabeth, the royal couple smiled pleasantly as they went down the receiving line. They went down the receiving line twice—because they had spotted Winston Churchill and moved right in on him. Mr. Churchill was gracious and shook their hands.

Family friends entertained them at a dinner or two in London, and after sight-seeing England they headed for Paris, a tour of the château country, a peek at Juan-les-Pins on the French Riviera (where they sighted Mr. Churchill again); Lucerne, Interlaken, and the Jungfrau in Switzerland; Milan, Venice, Florence, Rome; and then back to Paris by train.

At home after the six-week, tight-scheduled trip, Jacqueline longed to go back to Europe. On a Vassar bulletin board she found a notice about the Smith College groups which spent their junior year studying abroad. Though Vassar did not participate in the plan, she determined to join it. "If I could spend my junior year abroad!" she wrote to the dean.

Though it was unusual, the college authorities, because of her high grades, were amenable to having her join a group studying in England. But Jacqueline, her French heritage beckoning, wanted France only. To get there she would have to supplement her regular program with extra courses in French. Jacqueline was given permission to try. She passed with flying colors and in the late summer sailed away to study at the University of Grenoble, then the Sorbonne.

That summer of 1949 when the Smith College group, having voyaged nine days in cabin class, arrived in France, Jacqueline received a very special reception en route to Grenoble via Paris. At the Gare St. Lazare, a porter glimpsed her name on a luggage label. "Jacqueline!" he exclaimed, "C'est le nom de ma fille!" Jacqueline wrote her mother: "He kept calling me 'Mademoiselle Jacqueline' and talking all the way down the platform. Then I didn't see him for about twenty minutes. We got into the bus. And they piled the bags on top and I was sitting in back (way in back) and just before we pulled out he leapt on the bus and came running down the aisle asking 'Ou est Mlle. Jacqueline?' and he found me and ran up and shook hands and said 'Au revoir, Mademoiselle Jacqueline, je suis No. 27 si vous revenez' —to start off in a country with something friendly and gay like that made me love it—I really want to go back to the Gare St. Lazare to see numero 27."

During the summer session at the University of Grenoble Jacqueline lived with a French family and wrote home: ". . . they just grow on you so—They get nicer every day and open up to us and treat us like members of the family. We all laugh hysterically through meals and the mother is so good-natured. They are of the old aristocracy and hard up now and have to take in students."

French students helped the Americans in sympathetic camaraderie. Jacqueline wrote her mother: "They helped us with our compositions. I wrote mine in halting French and my friend did it all over. It really was very hard and they all took it so seriously and searched for words to use —it was really so nice of them to take all that trouble with some dumb foreigner who couldn't do her homework."

The students made a number of side trips in southern France. They went to Nîmes and Arles. Jacqueline described her joy in one of these expeditions:

I just can't tell you what it is like to come down from the mountains of Grenoble to this flat, blazing plain where seven-eighths of all you see is hot blue sky—and there are rows of poplars at the edge of every field to protect the crops from the mistral and spiky short palm trees with blazing red flowers growing at their feet. The people here speak with the lovely twang of the "accent du Midi." They are always happy as they live in the sun and love to laugh. It was heartbreaking to only get such a short glimpse of it all—I want to go back and soak it all up. The part I want to see is La Camargue—a land in the Rhône delta which is flooded by the sea every year and they have a ceremony where they all wade in on horses and bless it—La Bénédiction de la Mer—gypsies live there and bands of little Arab horses and they raise wild bulls.

On a Sunday they often explored the small villages near Grenoble:

Last Sunday we all went to Sassenage, a village on a plain near Grenoble. We visited the grottos and waded in underground rivers—and explored the town and sang songs and danced in a lovely little restaurant under rustling trees by a brook with a waterfall—the magic broken only by two "pièces de résistance" of the restaurant—"Bongo, Bongo, Bongo" and "Chattanooga Choo-choo." We missed the last tram and had to walk back to Grenoble (all the way back)—about five miles!

The Sorbonne specializes in teaching French civilization and French literature. Currently the most distinguished section of the University of Paris, its professors are world-famous. At first a theological school founded in 1250 by Robert de Sorbonne, private chaplain to Louis IX, the institution soon widened its scope to include philosophy. The school's most famous or, perhaps, infamous, academic judgment was proclaimed in 1431 when the Sorbonne sided with England in condemning Joan of

Arc. The Sorbonne retained its separate entity until 1808 when Napoleon arbitrarily handed it over to the University of Paris.

The original chapel is still in use and the more modern buildings are built on the old site which runs along the rue de la Sorbonne and branches into the Boulevard St. Michel. There are many foreigners among the twenty thousand or so enrolled students and in the winter of 1949–50, one of them was Jacqueline Bouvier.

Smith College girls stay in Reid Hall, a dormitory for American students. Jacqueline wanted to live with a French family where only French was spoken. So she became the paying guest of the Comtesse de Renty, a widow whose husband had disappeared in a concentration camp where she herself had been imprisoned. Comtesse de Renty had a tiny income and managed all the cooking for the seven who lived in her apartment. She spoke only a single word, "milk," in English. And she pronounced it "meelk." Jacqueline adored her and they still correspond.

Jacqueline wrote a letter to her step-brother Yusha describing the de Rentys. "They are the most wonderful family. I feel exactly as if I'm in my own house—heavenly mother—sort of like Mummy—Claude, daughter, my age—divorced daughter Ghislaine and her four year old son Christian—and two American girls who just finished Milton."

The Comtesse's apartment was freezing. Jacqueline did her homework in bed, muffled in scarf, mittens, sweater, and earmuffs! There was a single bathroom containing an antique tin tub for all seven people. Hot water was rare and so, enforcedly, Jacqueline took many cold showers that winter. One chilly day, when she was trying to take a hot bath, the water heater exploded and the resulting concussion shattered the bathroom window. Shortly after Jacqueline's husband was elected to the presidency, Comtesse de Renty, in a congratulatory letter, referred to this incident as assurance that Jacqueline would surmount the hazards of being First Lady. "Je sais les explosions de gaz ne vous font peur!"

That same winter Jacqueline's mother and stepfather came to Paris to see how she was getting along. They knew she cared surprisingly little for creature comforts. But she never once complained about the tin tub nor did she mention wearing mittens and earmuffs doing homework. They were pleased and proud.

Claude de Renty became one of her best friends. In the summer of 1950 they took an economy-style trip together. "I had the most terrific vacation in Austria and Germany," Jacqueline wrote her stepbrother Yusha. "We really saw what it was like with the Russians with Tommy guns in Vienna. We saw Vienna and Salzburg and Berchtesgarden where Hitler lived: Munich and the Dachau concentration camp—It's so much more fun travelling second and third class and sitting up all night in trains, as you really get to know people and hear their stories. When I travelled before it was all too luxurious and we didn't see anything."

Late in 1960 both Jacqueline and Claude were expecting babies. Mme. de Renty, in a letter written to Jacqueline before either baby was born, said: "We will hope for boys and that your husband and our general will ensure for them a more tranquil world."

As she continued to live in Paris Jacqueline's love for the beautiful city grew more understanding.

It is so different, the feeling you get in a city when you live there [she wrote Yusha]. I remember last summer when we were here—I thought Paris was all glamour and glitter and rush—but of course it isn't—I was so goggle-eyed at that night club you took me to. I went there the other night and it just seemed too garish. I really have two lives—flying from here (the de Renty apartment) to the Sorbonne and Reid Hall, in a lovely, quiet, rainy world—or, like the maid on her day out, putting on a fur coat and going to the middle of town and being swanky at the Ritz. But I really like the first part best. I have an absolute mania now about learning to speak French perfectly. We never speak a word of English in this apartment and I don't see many Americans.—The most wonderful thing here is all the operas and theatres and ballets and how easy they are to get to and how cheap—you could go out every night all winter and still not have seen everything that's playing.

I do love Paris and am so happy here but it is not the dazzled adoration for it I had the first time I saw it—a much more easy going and healthy affection this time.

That same year Jacqueline's mother saw an announcement in *Vogue* of the magazine's annual Prix de Paris, a contest open to young women and offering the winner a six-month job on *Vogue* in Paris and a similar span in New York plus some fancy trimmings. Janet tore out the notice and sent it to her daughter, saying it was something she thought Jacqueline would do well and find amusing.

Contestants had to submit four technical papers on fashion; a personal profile; the plan for a whole issue of *Vogue*; and five hundred words on "People I Wish I Had Known." Jacqueline, who had returned home after her year at the Sorbonne, was polishing off her College career at George Washington University. Simultaneously she worked hard on the contest. She won first prize. What intrigued the editors most was her choice of people she "wished she had known." None were political figures. They were Diaghilev, Oscar Wilde, Charles Baudelaire—respectively Russian ballet impressario, British author, and French poet.

Jacqueline, though winning first place, turned down the Prix de Paris awards. Her family thought she had been away from home long enough. She had spent two wonderful summers in Europe after her year at the Sorbonne. In 1950 she joined her stepbrother Yusha and traveled to Ireland (where she kissed the Blarney stone and inspected Dublin University) and across Scotland, through Auchincloss country, to its northernmost tip, a sharp spike of rocks called John o'Groat's. The second holiday she acted as mentor and guide to sister Lee on the latter's first trip abroad.

The two girls toured in a drive-yourself car from Paris to Spain and through Italy. Jacqueline celebrated her twenty-second birthday in Florence. There, at his enchanting villa outside the old city, they visited the great art critic and connoisseur, the late Bernard Berenson, whom Jacqueline considers one of the two most impressive people she ever met. The other is General de Gaulle.

Early in 1952 Jacqueline became the Inquiring Camera Girl on the Washington *Times-Herald,* now defunct. She got the job in a somewhat roundabout way. New York Times colmunist Arthur Krock telephoned Frank Waldrop, editor of the *Times-Herald,* and asked, "Are you still hiring little girls?"

Waldrop whose prewar secretary had been Kathleen Kennedy, very pretty sister of a bright young Harvard man named Jack Kennedy, replied in the affirmative.

"Well, I have a wonder for you," continued Krock.

"She's round-eyed, clever, and wants to go into journalism. Will you see her?"

Waldrop would. Shortly before Christmas Jacqueline went to Waldrop's office. "Do you want to go into journalism, or do you want to hang around here until you get married?" asked the editor sternly.

"No, sir!" replied Jacqueline humbly. "I want to make a career!"

"Well, if you're serious, I'll be serious," Waldrop continued more amiably, "if not, you can have a job clipping things."

"No, sir!" said Jacqueline even more humbly. "I'm serious." He told her to come back after the holidays. "Don't you come back to me in six months and say you're engaged!" was the newsman's parting shot. "No, SIR!" murmured Jacqueline.

The newspaper had published an Inquiring Photographer column for years, written and photographed by a man. The editor had always wanted a girl reporter to take over. It was a popular feature which Waldrop considered important and consisted of snapshotting eight or ten people daily, writing their answers to human-interest as well as topical-interest questions. The job did not merely provide a comment on the news but rather more insight into the way people felt. The questions might cover, for instance, interviewing a group of high school girls, asking them how they went about making their first date. Or, did those questioned think it made a boy look more mature if he parted his hair in the center? This sort of question took skill and sensitivity on the part of the interviewer not to ridicule or ham up. The column's interest depended on how expertly the interview was handled and not on the photographs. They were, in Waldrop's opinion, unimportant.

Inquiring Camera Girl
By JACQUELINE BOUVIER

THE QUESTION

What's it like observing the pages at close range? Asked of senators and the Vice President.

THE ANSWERS

Vice President Richard M. Nixon: I would predict that some future statesman will come from the ranks of the page corps. During my time as a senator, I noticed that they are very quick boys, most of whom have a definite interest in politics. I feel they could  not get a better political grounding than by witnessing the Senate in session day after day as they do.

Sen. John F. Kennedy (D) of Massachusetts: I've often thought that the country might be better off if we Senators and the pages traded jobs. If such legislation is ever enacted I'll be glad to hand over the reins to Jerry Hoobler. In the meantime, I 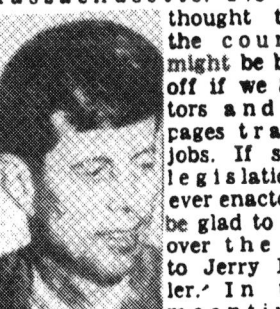 think he might be just the fellow to help me straighten out my relationship with the cops. I've often mistaken Jerry for a senator because he looks so old.

THE QUESTION

What's it like observing senators at close range? Asked of Senate pages.

THE ANSWERS

Gary Hegelson, Wisconsin: We've got this book with pictures of senators in it and I'm trying to get their autographs. I didn't know when I could get Nixon, he's so busy. One day when he was presiding over the Senate and I was sitting on the rostrum I decided  that was my chance. He signed it right away.

Jerry Hoobler of Ohio: Senator Kennedy always brings his lunch in a brown paper bag. I guess he eats it in his office. I see him with it every morning when I'm on the elevator. He's always being mistaken for a tourist by the cops because he looks so young.  The other day he wanted to use the special phones, and they told him, "Sorry, mister, but these are reserved for senators."

Inquiring Camera Girl by Jacqueline Bouvier. (COURTESY OF WASHINGTON TIMES-HERALD)

Jacqueline assured the editor that she could handle a camera. So she was given the job. She did know how to handle a camera—a Brownie or Leica—but not a cumbersome, professional photographer's Graflex. Undaunted, Jacqueline, always competent and self-sufficient, merely turned to the classified telephone directory, picked out a photography school, made an appointment, then dropped in to learn her new trade.

After a brief tour of police stations and hospitals to learn what city life was like, Jacqueline was on her own. Her first week's pay check was the dazzling sum of $42.50. It looked big, for a moment, because the only other money she had earned was a minuscule fee paid by *Life* magazine when she appeared, far in the background, as one of many models in a Vassar charity fashion show. She was given a number of small raises and before long was earning $56.75 a week.

Waldrop sized her up favorably: "She was a businesslike little girl—nice, quiet, concentrated, obviously very, very earnest in wanting to be a professional. She was self-sufficient, good at listening and she handled her job efficiently."

Though Jacqueline always preferred doing columns on such favorite subjects as ballet dancers or children ("Children always give better answers than anyone," she claims), her most talked-about efforts concerned public personalities.

One day the editor sent Jacqueline up on the Hill to do a column about the new members of Congress, among them John Fitzgerald Kennedy, a former Massachusetts representative who had recently achieved a sensational victory by defeating well-entrenched Senator Henry Cabot Lodge. Waldrop knew Kennedy well and liked him. But he had heard rumors that his Inquiring Camera Girl had been "seeing" him quite often.

"Go up on the Hill and see this fellow," he ordered. "Tell him I sent you." Then he added, "You behave yourself. Don't get your hopes up. He's too old for you—besides, he doesn't want to get married."

Jacqueline rolled her eyes, said nothing, and went off on her assignment. Later that week she lugged her Graflex up on the Hill again. This time the "victims" were two Senate pages, two members of Congress, Vice President Nixon and Massachusetts Senator John F. Kennedy. Jacqueline asked the pages, "What's it like observing senators at close range?" and conversely, to the Vice President and the Senator, "What's it like observing the pages at close range?"

The answers were inconsequential but fun. In retrospect, the juxtaposition of the principles, was prophetic.

For years Charlie Bartlett, Washington correspondent for the New York *Times* owned Chattanooga *Times*, had been trying to get Jacqueline and his friend Jack together. Before his marriage to Martha, a handsome redhead, Barlett took Jacqueline out occasionally. He soon decided that Jackie-and-Jack were made for each other. But each proved elusive as quicksilver. Once, at the wedding of Charlie's sister they were both actually in the same room. But Jack stood in one corner, dead-seriously talking politics, while Jacqueline was in another, surrounded by young men. Neither could be diverted or detached. Another time Charlie almost made it. Both were asked to a Bartlett family christening but Congressman Kennedy never showed up.

Charlie, a Chicagoan and Yale man, smart, fun, and awfully nice, had met Jack Kennedy after the war when his family wintered at Hobe Sound and the Kennedys were practically next door at Palm Beach. Charlie gravitated to Washington, launched into journalism and became fast friends with the tyro Massachusetts legislator. Soon Bartlett and Kennedy had much in common, for both won Pulitzer prizes. The Senator was tapped for his book *Profiles in Courage* and the journalist for his scoop in disclosing government irregularities in the Air Force Administration. Eventually, the Bartletts and the Kennedys became so close that Jack Kennedy acted as godfather to the Bartlett's daughter and Martha Bartlett served as godmother to the Kennedys' son.

In June 1951, the just-married Bartletts succeeded as match-makers. They gave a dinner for eight in their tiny Georgetown house. After dinner the guests sat in the handkerchief-sized back yard talking and when it was time to leave, both the host and the Congressman escorted Jacqueline to her car. But Josie, the Bartletts' fox terrier got there first. The Congressman had been murmuring to Jacqueline something about "coming out for a drink," when Josie hopped in the open car door. With shrill barks she pounced on a man sitting in the back seat. He was a beau of Jacqueline's who had recognized her black Mercury and stepped in to wait for her! This evidence of devotion froze Representative Kennedy and he made himself scarce. Shortly afterwards Jacqueline sailed with sister Lee for a summer in Europe.

Next winter when she was working for the *Times-Herald* Congressman Kennedy was busy mending political fences in preparation for his senatorial contest. The first time they went out together he took her dancing in the Shoreham Hotel's Blue Room. But they weren't a two-some. A political friend from Massachusetts came along, although he had very hard sledding conversationally. After that, because both were so well known in Washington, they never went out together to public places.

During the summer of 1952 Jacqueline, working on the *Times-Herald*, saw little of Jack.

As Inquiring Camera Girl on a Washington newspaper, Jacqueline interviewed bus drivers, ballet dancers, children, VIPs. "Don't get your hopes up," her boss warned Jacqueline when he assigned her to see Senator John F. Kennedy. Here she is snapping a London bus driver, one of a group taking a busman's holiday in the United States.

After Congress convened in January the new Senator and the Inquiring Camera Girl courted strictly out of public gaze. They dined with friends and family and took in an occasional movie.

Their courtship followed a curious, private pattern. They dined often alone with the Bartletts and filled the evening with carefree bridge, Chinese checkers, and sometimes Monopoly. Or they would dine and occasionally go to a movie with Bobby and Ethel Kennedy. The only time they had any real privacy was when Jack would drive Jacqueline back along the Potomac and over Key Bridge to Merrywood. One night his car broke down halfway out the long driveway which twists through the woods and over a narrow, rustic bridge. Jack came tramping back to the house, where Jacqueline gave him the keys to Uncle Hugh's car. Next morning Uncle Hugh was quite surprised to find his shiny vehicle gone and a broken-down automobile with a Massachusetts license plate blocking his drive.

At eleven P.M. on a Wednesday evening early in May 1953, Aileen Bowdoin, older sister of two of the girls with whom Jacqueline made her first trip to Europe, telephoned her, "How would you like to go to the Coronation?" she asked.

They would have to sail two days later on the Queen Mary! Somehow they made it, arriving on board with not a clue as to where they would stay in crowded London. But everything straightened out on the gala voyage. Friends of their parents rallied around; they were loaned an apartment, found fine seats for the Coronation procession, were invited to the United States Embassy, to dinners and to Perle Mesta's jumbo dance. Even suitable escorts were provided.

Jacqueline reported the great event. Her stories and quick, catchy one-line sketches were front-paged in the *Times-Herald*. She sketched everything from the Duke and Duchess of Windsor's dogs kenneled on the Queen Mary to a triangular impasse at Perle Mesta's ball involving Lauren Bacall, Humphrey Bogart, and the Marquess of Milford Haven. She roamed the streets interviewing American tourists, British housewives, Cockney laborers, students from Caribbean islands. Her vivid account of what she saw was a genuine journalistic success. Every possible moment when she wasn't working or attending some Coronation festivity she was poking around in bookstores. She bought books and more books and was very

Senator Kennedy and his fiancée pictured on a magazine cover shortly after their engagement was announced in the summer of 1953. They are sailing on the Senator's twenty-four-foot sailboat VICTURA *at Hyannis Port.* (HY PESKIN)

mysterious when Aileen asked about her purchases. When, after a week of fun in Paris, the girls flew home, Jacqueline had to pay over a hundred dollars in excess fare for the heavy, book-filled suitcase. The volumes, mostly on history and legislation were a present, of course, for Senator Kennedy.

The returning plane was scheduled to touch down in Boston before arriving in New York. Aileen hoped a beau would meet her, and so did Jacqueline. They grew increasingly nervous as they neared the United States coast line and made a last-minute rush to primp. But the powder room had been pre-empted by Zsa Zsa Gabor, who held the fort until the plane was ready to land. Aileen and Jacqueline walked down the gangway with shiny noses.

Inside, in the waiting room, leaning casually against a counter, was Senator John Fitzgerald Kennedy.

"Aunt Maudie," said a voice over the long-distance wire, "I just want you to know that I'm engaged to Jack Kennedy." It was Jacqueline, calling one of her father's twin sisters. "But you can't tell anyone for a while," she went on, "because it wouldn't be fair to *The Saturday Evening Post*."

"What," asked puzzled Aunt Maudie, "has *The Saturday Evening Post* to do with your engagement?"

"*The Post* is coming out tomorrow," laughed Jackie, "with an article on Jack. And the title is on the cover. It's 'Jack Kennedy—the Senate's Gay Young Bachelor.'"

Part Three

Formal announcement of the engagement was postponed. It would have been unforgivable to proclaim the impending defection of the "Gay Young Bachelor" from celibacy while the magazine was still on sale!

The bridegroom-to-be's personality was engagingly thumb-nailed in the article. "Kennedy appears to be a walking fountain of youth. He is six feet tall, lean, of hard physique and has the innocently respectful face of an altar boy at High Mass. He is 'Nature Boy' with an Ivy League polish, but his exterior nonchalance conceals a terrific will to win." Then, attempting to capture the elusive Kennedy appeal, the article concluded, "... and it is said that during the campaign every woman who met Kennedy wanted to mother him or to marry him."

Jacqueline was no exception. The evening they had been introduced Jacqueline looked into Jack's laughingly aroused, intelligently inquisitive face and knew instantly that he would have a profound, perhaps a disturbing influence on her life. In a flash of inner perception she realized that here was a man who did not want to marry. She was frightened. Jacqueline, in this revealing moment, envisaged heartbreak, but just as swiftly determined such heartbreak would be worth the pain.

Jacqueline was right. The Massachusetts congressman did not want to marry then. But a year later when they became engaged Jack confided he had decided that night to marry her. He wished to wait awhile, but when he was ready she would be the one. (Jacqueline's snappy answering comment: "How *big* of you!")

Senator Kennedy and his bride on the lawn of Hammersmith Farm, Newport, shortly after their marriage in St. Mary's Church, September 13, 1953, three months after they became engaged.
(© TONI FRISSELL)

That warm June evening in 1951, on the brick sidewalk outside the Bartletts' house, these two who were so irrevocably drawn to each other, parted. They did not meet again for seven months.

The congressman from Massachusetts had a big job to do campaigning against an established veteran opponent, Senator Henry Cabot Lodge. Throughout the land there was a Republican landslide, but the young Democrat who "at first glance looked a little lonesome and in need of a haircut and perhaps a square meal" defeated his adversary by a staggering 69,060 votes.

That same summer Jacqueline lugged her clumsy Graflex camera around torrid Washington, patiently lining up victims for her Inquiring Girl column. In September she vacationed briefly, accompanying her mother and stepfather to a bankers' conference in Mexico. They weekended in Acapulco, where Jacqueline fell in love with a charming house. It was pink and staggered up from the turquoise sea on varying levels against a rosy-tan cliff. Jacqueline thought she would like to spend her honeymoon in it. Miraculously, two years later Mrs. John Fitzgerald Kennedy did!

Twenty-four-year-old Jacqueline Lee Bouvier and thirty-six-year-old Senator John Fitzgerald Kennedy were married September 12, 1953, three months after they became engaged.

The night before their wedding, at the bridal dinner in Newport's Clambake Club, the bridegroom, in a tongue-in-cheek speech, disclosed why he was relinquishing his bachelorhood. His motivation, he said, was to remove his bride from the Fourth Estate. She had become too smart a reporter and, as Inquiring Camera Girl, menaced his political future.

The bride teased back. As a suitor, she stated solemnly,

Senator John Fitzgerald Kennedy and his bride dancing under a striped marquee at their wedding reception at Hammersmith Farm, Newport, residence of Mrs. Kennedy's step father and mother, Mr. and Mrs. Hugh Dudley Auchincloss. (© TONI FRISSELL)

Mrs. John Fitzgerald Kennedy throwing her bridal bouquet, a charming combination of tiny spray orchids, stephanotis, and miniature gardenias. (© TONI FRISSELL)

the Senator was in some way a failure. Though famed for literary profusion he had penned no romantic love letters and in fact, had dispatched to her only a single written communication. She then held aloft for bridesmaids and ushers to see a Bermuda-postmarked card. On one side was a scarlet hibiscus blossom, on the other a tender legend: "Wish you were here. Jack."

Five days before the ceremony, which attracted thousands of well-wishers to St. Mary's Church in Newport, the Joseph Kennedys invited the ten bridesmaids and fourteen ushers to a glorified house party in Hyannis Port. Some of the bridal party were family. The others stayed in a rented house across the street from the "Kennedy Compound." True to rugged Kennedy tradition, the guests were propelled into a tight schedule of tennis, touch football, swimming, sailing, picnicking. In the evenings there were a scavenger hunt and charades. Everyone had to contribute; the Kennedys let no one escape. Highlights included the senior Mr. Kennedy's birthday. Each of his "children" gave him a sweater and popped them, one atop another, over his head.

The bridegroom was gay and happy to be with his old friends. His "leadership" showed, pals noticed, only when he skippered his ancient twenty-four-foot sailboat, *Victura*. Then he became serious, competitive, impatient with his landlubbers.

Everyone left Hyannis Port for the bridal dinner given at the Clambake Club by the bride's mother and stepfather. There, on the eve of the wedding, the bridal attendants received their gifts. The Senator presented Brooks Brothers umbrellas to his groomsmen. Jacqueline gave her bridesmaids monogrammed silver picture frames.

The wedding day was warm, bright, and so windy it ruffled the bride's hair and disarranged flowers decorating the flock of small tables set for hundreds invited to the luncheon reception at Hammersmith Farm.

The bridesmaids wore pale pink taffeta with claret-color sashes, Lee as matron of honor, was girdled in deeper pink. But it was six-year-old Jamie Auchincloss, not the pretty girls, who stole the show. In short black velvet trousers and jaboted white silk shirt, he performed as page with comically grave Old World courtesy.

The bride's gown was a fairy-princess's dream of taffeta faille, creamy white to blend with the faintly yellowed rose-point-lace veil lent by Jacqueline's grandmother, Mrs. James T. Lee. Each panel of the swooping skirt was swirled with a rosette, centered by an orange-blossom sprig. The lace veil, shirred into a back-of-the-head cap spiked with orange blossoms, flowed to the ground. She borrowed her mother's lace handkerchief, wore a blue garter, pridefully displayed a handsome diamond bracelet—the bridegroom's gift—and her engagement ring, a twinned square-cut emerald and diamond. She carried an unpretentious bouquet of tiny spray orchids, stephanotis, and miniature gardenias. Jacqueline, as a bride, looked adorable.

Six hundred guests packed St. Mary's Church, Archbishop Cushing, who offered the invocation at President Kennedy's inaugural, officiated at the marriage ceremony, and His Holiness, the Pope, conferred an apostolic blessing. Back at Hammersmith Farm, Meyer Davis, who had played at the wedding of Jacqueline's parents, fiddled gaily away. Upstairs literally thousands of wedding presents were displayed. Downstairs the tiered wedding cake was a conversation piece. It was the gift of a Kennedy admirer, a baker whose original plan was to represent an "ocean of love" as a large square of cake topped with icing waves and dotted with doves. He had

Senator and Mrs. John Fitzgerald Kennedy cutting their wedding cake. On the bridegroom's left, the bride's sister Lee, now Princess Stanislas Radziwill of London. (© TONI FRISSELL)

been coaxed into a more maneuverably edible pattern by the bride's mother!

After the last toast was pledged and the bridal bouquet tossed, the bride reappeared in a trim gray suit, carrying her emerald velvet hat because she imagined it unbecoming. In a flurry of rice Senator and Mrs. Kennedy left for their honeymoon in the pink house on the rosy-tan cliff above the turquoise sea at Acapulco.

It had been a wonderful wedding.

Jacqueline, who from her teens had lived in a household which included seven children of varying ages and temperaments, was now part of a larger, extraordinarily united family. "The Kennedys are the most welcoming family," she says. "The day you become engaged to one of them is the day they start saying how 'fantastic' you are." ("Fantastic" is a favorite Kennedy word which they have appropriated to underscore special Kennedy approval. Kennedys never use the word in its correct dictionary meaning, i.e., "grotesque, quaint; whimsical; extravagantly fanciful.") "And the same loyalty they show to each other they show to their in-laws," she continued. "They are all so proud when one of them does well."

Each Kennedy has some special attribute which the others extol, Jacqueline notes. Jack is Jack. (Even Kennedys can't extol a superlative.) Bobby has the best legal mind in the country. Sargent Shriver and Eunice are the most civic-minded. Ethel (Bobby's wife) is "fantastic" because of her energy, seven children and incredible efficiency. Pat Lawford is the smartest; Peter, the best of actors. Jean is the most domestic, and Steve, her husband, the one with the best business head. Teddy is the best natural politician. His wife, Joan, is the most beautiful. Her mother-in-law, Mrs. Kennedy, is the most

At Hammersmith Farm after the ceremony. In the wedding picture Mrs. Kennedy's sister Lee and nine-year-old half-sister Janet, are seated directly in front of her; step-brother Yusha is at far right. Charles Bartlett, who introduced the bride and groom, stands at far left. (© TONI FRISSELL)

devout. Jackie is Jackie and, of course, the most well-read.

Jacqueline can never decide which Kennedy she likes the best. She "adores" her father-in-law and, among "the children," is closest to Jean Smith because Caroline Kennedy and Jean's son, Stephen, are of an age and devoted to each other. "Someday they may elope and cause a scandal," says Jacqueline with a twinkle. But Bobby Kennedy is "the one I would put my hand in the fire for." To her, next to Jack, he is the most "fantastic" Kennedy.

The love and security of being part of such a close-knit clan was bliss to Jacqueline. When it came time to choose a house for the summer, the Senator thought of going somewhere within easy commuting distance from Washington. It was Jacqueline, not Jack, who made the decision to move into the Kennedy Compound in Hyannis Port. She wanted her children to grow up with all their Kennedy cousins and enjoy the same warm assurance as did their Kennedy fathers and mothers. Caroline, to Jacqueline's delight, acts as well as looks pure Kennedy. To make her proud of her name and live up to it, when Caroline hurts herself her mother says sternly, "Kennedys don't cry." Usually, but not always—since Caroline is developing into a decided individualist—this stops Miss Kennedy's wails.

The first years of their marriage the Kennedys lived either in rented houses or those belonging to their parents. There was so much excitement. They were always going somewhere—to Europe, to make a speech, to attend some political function. "It was hectic, but I rather enjoyed it," Jacqueline remembers. "You don't really long for a home of your own unless you have children." Occasionally excitement had its disadvantages. "I soon learned to pack quickly and go anywhere," Jacqueline says, "but

Jacqueline Bouvier Kennedy. This photograph was taken during the summer of 1960 and, to date, is President Kennedy's favorite picture of his wife. (© JACQUES LOWE)

sometimes the one pair of shoes I needed vitally were left in a trunk in the basement of Merrywood—just when I'd be in Boston!"

That first winter Jacqueline went back to school. She studied American history at the Georgetown School of Foreign Service, partly because she knew so little about it but mostly because her husband knew so much. She "adored" it and, as usual, studying hard, nailed down her subject, which she found rewarding as a springboard into political life. (For leisure reading Jacqueline still prefers European history. Its complexities appeal to her very feminine taste. "American history is for men," she claims.)

Later her languages, which she continued to polish, came in handy to her husband. It was summer, 1955; they were dining at the United States Embassy in Rome. Clare Boothe Luce presided as Ambassador, and Georges Bidault, former French Prime Minister, was a starred guest. After dinner, among the men, the Minister and the Senator wanted to talk, but Kennedy's French was shaky and Bidault's English almost nonexistent. So Jacqueline was summoned to act as interpreter. Afterward M. Bidault wrote her a delightful letter saying with gallant accuracy, "Jamais je n'ai vue autant de sagesse reveti d'autant de grace." ("I have never seen so much wisdom adorned with so much charm.")

Jacqueline accompanied her husband on many speaking trips, mainly to Massachusetts. The first time she campaigned around the clock was in 1958, when the Senator sought a second term. "I'm so glad Jack comes from Massachusetts," she exclaims, "because it is the state with the most history. Driving from one rally to another, we'd pass John Quincy Adams's house or Harvard—or Plymouth. I think I know every corner of Massachusetts. I'm glad I've had a chance to see the whole state. We spent that election night in Boston, and of course Jack won by the most incredible majority—and we were so happy!"

(Senator Kennedy was re-elected by an 870,000 majority during the Republican Administration of President Eisenhower.)

These first married years were saddened by the Senator's near-fatal illness and Jacqueline's difficulties in having children. These shared troubles helped knit them closer. They both longed for children. But there had been a miscarriage in 1955. The next year, by emergency Caesarean section, her baby was born dead a month prematurely. The stress of the 1956 national convention, at which the Senator lost the nomination for Vice President by an eyelash, had been too great; it was touch and go whether Jacqueline would survive.

When Caroline came the day after 1957 Thanksgiving, her safe arrival seemed so incredible that Jacqueline would try to stay awake at night to banish sleep as long as she could so that she might savor in extra minutes how happy she was and how overwhelmingly she loved her baby girl and Jack.

Jacqueline had undergone two Caesareans and faced a third for the baby who was to be born at Christmas 1960, the vital, presidential-election year. She was torn between determination to help her husband become President and mortal fear that any extra effort would cost her this passionately desired child.

She left nothing undone that was in her capacity to do. She personally penned thousands of letters and wrote a weekly newspaper column called "Campaign Wife" which reached Kennedy workers across the land. She conferred with women leaders on questions of feminine importance and gave full-dress press conferences in

The President's daughter "looks and acts pure Kennedy." She was one year old when this nursery photograph was taken. (© JACQUES LOWE)

Hyannis Port, then in Washington. Though her baby was expected in weeks, she appeared on TV shows and at TV fund-raising teas.

Only those who knew her well realized how much Jacqueline undertook and at what cost to her. The New York ticker-tape parade, riding perched on the back of an open car beside her husband, almost undid her. As their automobile progressed at snail's pace through the financial district enthusiasts, estimated at two million, rushed the police lines, stopped the car several times, and almost toppled it in their eagerness to shake hands with the Kennedys. It was one of the great moments of John Fitzgerald Kennedy's life, but terrifying to his wife. She knew her strength had been overtaxed. A few weeks later when John Fitzgerald Kennedy, Jr. decided to arrive a month ahead of schedule, only a matter of minutes, luck, and a wonderful doctor saved him.

Jack Kennedy's back trouble started, in characteristic Kennedy fashion, through the rigors of family competition. His elder, adored brother, Joe, had made the Harvard varsity football team. The lighter, less swift-of-foot, younger brother achieved only the junior varsity. Jack tried so hard, played with such crazy courage Sophomore year that he incurred a presumed ruptured disk in his lower spine. This injury, never cured, was reactivated when a Japanese destroyer, slicing in half the PT boat Jack commanded, slammed him onto the deck. Afterward, saving the survivors, he towed a badly burned crewman three chilly miles to shore, holding the belt of his life jacket between clenched teeth during five aching hours. For days afterward Lieutenant Kennedy swam back and forth to nearby islands, seeking and eventually effecting rescue. Exhausted by this effort, he developed sciatica and a severe case of malaria which lingered seven years.

Lieutenant Kennedy, for whom a memorial service had been held in the Pacific, returned to convalesce in the United States, weighing a mere 127 pounds and suffering agonizing spinal pain. At a Massachusetts naval hospital in the spring of 1944 he underwent a lumbar-disc operation to remove pressure on the sciatic nerve and thus terminate a muscular spasm.

Years later (in 1955) Dr. Janet Travell, now the first woman White House doctor in history, discovered that one of Mr. Kennedy's legs was a bit longer than the other. Usually such trifling differences are equalized by the body, but when there has been a muscle spasm this can become a constant irritant. In walking, the uneven lengths cause a seesaw motion which strains the spinal muscles and encourages any spasm originating from an old injury. (Today President Kennedy wears a quarter-inch lift in his left heel and on occasion a flexible, corset-like brace as a back support.)

Despite the 1944 operation, interminable hours on his feet during the 1950 and 1952 campaigns caused recurrence of the muscular spasm. The first summer of their marriage when the Kennedys were living at Merrywood the pain had grown so severe that the Senator took to crutches for relief. He lost weight, tipped the scales at a scary 140 pounds, and seemed to be melting away. His resistance was so unsure that the doctors couldn't determine whether to operate again or not. The Senator himself decided to risk surgery rather than endure such continuing agony.

On October 21, 1954, scarcely a year after their wedding, Jacqueline accompanied her husband to New York's Hospital for Special Surgery, where a lumbar spine operation was attempted. The operation was a failure. Infection set in and the Senator grew so desperately ill that family and staff members were alerted at midnight. It was believed that he might not live until morning and the last rites were administered. But he battled gamely and, though still in great pain, improved sufficiently to be flown on a stretcher to Palm Beach for Christmas.

The Senator came north again in six weeks to undergo a second—and this time successful—operation. He left the hospital, to return from Florida in April for a checkup. Then Senator Kennedy was referred to Dr. Travell, who discovered his leg discrepancy. She also cured his muscular spasms with Novocain which, injected directly, rapidly relaxed the cramped muscles, restoring them to their original length and thus causing them to function normally.

During these trying hospital sieges Jacqueline, in neverending attendance, lived in New York with Jack's sister Jean (now Mrs. Stephen Smith). When he was critically ill he was cared for authoritatively by nurses, but when he began to get better it was difficult to bolster the morale of so active a person. "I think convalescence is harder to bear than great pain," Jacqueline says. "He was so brave always."

She tried in every imaginable way to bolster his spirits. She read to him. She took time to poke in old bookstores for curious tomes which would pique his interest. She brought him idiotic presents to coax a smile. They staged, *à deux*, poetry-learning contests. When he was well enough, she lured old friends and fun people to his hospital room. Her most sensational coup was trapping Grace Kelly. They met at a small dinner. It was before Jack had received visitors, and nights he was understandably depressed by the elderly, after-dark nursing crew.

So when Grace asked how the Senator was, Jacqueline had a brilliant inspiration. Grace returned with her to the hospital, then tapped on the patient's door. When he answered grumpily she walked in, announcing, "I'm the new night nurse!" A glimpse of dazzling Grace boosted her "patient's" temperature, pulse, and morale sky-high!

Down in Palm Beach, the Senator found time in bed hanging heavy. He commenced writing and painting. A year or so before he had read the story of Kansas Senator Edmund Ross, a promising young man who served his first senatorial term just after the Civil War. Ross deliberately committed political suicide by voting, against powerful pressures, according to the dictates of his judgment for what he considered "the highest good of the country." His single vote prevented President Andrew Johnson from being unjustly impeached.

Ross's courageous, almost-forgotten act intrigued the Senator, and from it stemmed his idea of discovering other such incidents and gathering them into a book. So he cranked up his hospital bed, asked the Library of Congress to express him innumerable books, and went to work. He found seven other senators whom he five-starred for political courage, and a handful of others, brave, but less conspicuously so. These true tales were melded together, interpreted by the Senator, and rounded out with his own personal philosophy of politics and courage. The result, *Profiles in Courage*, was a best seller and Pulitzer-prize winner.

Profiles in Courage couldn't have happened without Jacqueline. She encouraged her husband, read to him, carried out independent research and, on lined yellow copy paper, wrote down parts of the book. Her husband, listing thank-you credits in the preface, concluded: "This book would not have been possible without the encouragement, assistance and criticisms offered from the very beginning by my wife, Jacqueline, whose help during all the days of my convalescence I cannot ever adequately acknowledge."

Before attempting *Profiles in Courage,* the Senator had had another best seller under his belt, *Why England Slept,* an enlarged college thesis published in 1940. But, though he was a literary success already, he was a complete novice at painting. Nevertheless, he started turning out creditable landscapes. He sloshed away earnestly in bed, using his wife's painting equipment until his mother, appalled by mounting laundry problems, made him desist till he was well enough to sit in a chair in the more readily cleanable bathroom! He has scarcely wet a brush since, but those knowledgeable in art believe that Jack Kennedy could become a first-class painter.

The Senator returned to the Senate in May. He had been away almost eight months. During this span he had written a Pulitzer-Prize book, painted a number of excellent pictures, conquered a distressing injury and, more important, through pain had gained new depth of character and perception. Jacqueline, too, had changed. She was more tender, more understanding, and more of a woman. For the Kennedys, truly these eight months had not been wasted.

John Fitzgerald Kennedy says that the above is a picture of Jack and Jackie. He is the straight line and Jacqueline the ups and downs. "He is a rock," says his wife, "and I lean on him in everything. He is so kind. (Ask anyone who works for him!) And he's never irritable or sulky. He would do anything I wanted or give me anything I wanted."

When Caroline hurts herself, her mother says sternly, "Kennedys don't cry." Usually, but not always—since Caroline is developing into a distinct individualist—this stops Miss Kennedy's wails. Above, she is two, and pictured the summer before her father was elected to the presidency. (© JACQUES LOWE)

The ups and downs represent Jacqueline's many-faceted character which never ceases to charm her husband. She amuses him enormously and can always make him laugh, as he can her. He never could "get mad" with her. Before marriage Jack Kennedy was probably far too busy to give much thought to a woman's mind or emotions. Now, in Jacqueline, he admires both. And especially her self-sufficiency in maintaining an inner life of her own, devoted to her children, books, her drawing and painting, which keeps her content, though not happy, when he is away. He is lost without her. (Though, obviously, he does not moon about her in the heat of a campaign!) Old friends, used to bachelor-day fun, take note that should Jacqueline leave the room, their pal is likely to keep his eye peeled on the door, to tap his teeth with a pencil, and query restlessly, "Where's Jackie?"

For Jacqueline has brought beauty, laughter, and order into her husband's life. Beauty, not only in her person but in the lovely "things" she surrounds them with: flowers used simply; French drawings; graceful furniture; fragile china and embroidered linens; softly colored fabrics; charming bibelots, each with some special appeal. Laughter, for with her wit few can be more amusing with less effort. Order, the main factor missing from his bachelor life, once a continual rushing to planes and on the fly, grabbing hot dogs, malteds, candy bars. Jacqueline has cocooned him smoothly, running his house, conjuring delicious food, seeing to his clothes, getting him places, all with efficient unobtrusiveness. This protectiveness has notably improved his health, buoyed his energy, and made possible even more phenomenal Kennedy accomplishments. All this Jack Kennedy now appreciates.

What John Fitzgerald Kennedy brought into his wife's life is an all-encompassing—a *raison d'etre*. Her only resentment: she sees too little of him, and he is so often telephoning when she wants to talk to him!

When Jacqueline learned she was to have her first baby the Kennedys bought Hickory Hill, just a bit down the road from Merrywood. It was a fine spot, complete with orchard, stable, swimming pool plus a cheerful nursery, all spick-and-spanned by Jacqueline. Hickory Hill was made for a family and, without the eagerly awaited child, it was sad and lonely for Jacqueline. So they sold it to brother Bobby and his Ethel as home for their astronomically increasing brood. The Senator and his wife moved back into Georgetown, lived in a rented place until they found their red brick, slant-set Federal dream house. They moved in when Caroline was three weeks old.

The front door opened smack onto the sidewalk. Inside there was a long, high-ceilinged double-fireplaced drawing room. An inner window looked on the bricked back yard, shaded by shiny-leaved magnolia trees. Down the narrow hall were the dining room and a tiny passageway anteroom. Jacqueline painted the broad-planked old floors white with an overlying diamond pattern in pale green. The caned Louis XVI dining chairs repeated this white-and-green motif. French porcelain was displayed on the shelves, and "tieing" the small room together was a delightful carpet woven with strips of red roses. The Kennedys did a lot of living in their soothing, amiable drawing room which mirrored Jacqueline's love of eighteenth-century France. There were a few fragile Louis XV chairs, but mostly comfortable furniture, palest green upholstered. There were candle fitted *doré* wall fixtures, blonde wood marquetry tables and a variety of charming things—pink-glit porcelain cups and saucers used for cigarettes and as ash trays, Caroline's gold-belled coral

During the 1960 campaign Mrs. Kennedy wrote a weekly column, appeared on TV shows, and painted for relaxation. Above, she is painting in a bedroom in her Hyannis Port house. (© JACQUES LOWE)

baby rattle and, on the mantel, Jacqueline's pride and joy, a small French clock balanced on a complacent bronze lion, flanked by twin urns.

The Kennedys' joint loves were reflected in a Boudin painting of distant sailboats, a set of Vernet drawings, rows of giant books on painters—El Greco, Renoir, Picasso. There were many flowers, mostly generous bouquets of seasonable blossoms, often red or white tulips set in dramatic provincial copper pots.

During the past three years, as the Senator stepped up his pace toward the presidency, the Kennedys evolved a design for living based on Jacqueline's belief that her husband's incredible energy must be replenished by good food and plenty of sleep. Her most publicized device for keeping her husband properly fed was to dispatch luncheons to his office on a covered hot plate. These hot plates, identical to the nickel-and-china affairs used by Caroline, contained the same baby fare—peas-chop-potatoey meals—prepared in the Kennedy kitchen. They proved so tempting that the Senator abandoned his habit of snatching a midday sandwich or nibbling a candy bar. Friends liked the baby hot plates, too, and often George, the Senator's butler and right bower for over a decade, hustled three or four from N Street to Capitol Hill.

Weekday evenings the Senator and his wife seldom left home, often were alone, occasionally invited a few friends to dine. In a city where entertaining is a major business, Jacqueline went to formal social functions so infrequently that for several years she did not own a single long evening gown.

"Weekends when most people were relaxing," Jacqueline explained, "Jack worked hardest." For three years previous to his ultimate campaign he crisscrossed the country, speaking almost everywhere he was invited (back in 1959 he received around 10,000 invitations to speak) and finding out how the country responded to his ideas.

"For instance, we might fly to Oregon for three or four days," Jacqueline reminisced. "Then we would get up at six-thirty and go to breakfasts, luncheons, dinners in different places. Once in Wisconsin we drove fifty miles in below-zero weather and had to leave our car at two or three stops along the way. Urban areas were easier. There was usually an early press conference, a speech, a TV appearance and not much traveling." Jacqueline went on most of these trips. She learned to travel light. She took along a suit, a wool dress, a dressier dress with a jacket to ward off drafts at banquets.

The campaign night which she remembers most vividly was the one when her husband was nominated for the presidency. He was in Los Angeles; she was in Hyannis Port. Throughout the interminable evening she sat in a straight-backed chair painting with furious concentration. Her mother and stepfather were with her. They watched the TV and relayed a running account of what was happening. From time to time Jacqueline would drop her brush to see as well as hear the excitement. They stayed near the set until five A.M. Jacqueline finished her painting, a pixyish interpretation of the Senator's triumphant return to Hyannis Port. Next morning at ten, fresher than any daisy, she presided at her first press conference as potential First Lady.

When they are alone the Kennedys read incessantly. The President, always widening his scope in history and politics, never wastes time on Westerns or whodunits. The Pulitzer-prize winner often turns to Pitt, Fox, or Burke's orations for knowledge and help in his speeches. The new First Lady's special reading pattern is the eighteenth century, with emphasis on that century in France. She developed this interest living in Paris and during her travels. Through these past busy years she has kept on studying her favorite period and now believes she knows more about the eighteenth century than of any other subject.

Caroline, too, has become somewhat of an eighteenth-century buff, for occasionally her mother reads to her from a marvelous picture book glamorizing Louis XIV. She talks about Le Roi Soleil as if he were Peter Rabbit, and her favorite likeness of the elegant monarch is one on horseback, bedizened with plumes. Once Caroline, calling on elders, spotted a liquor bottle with a label sporting a gorgeously uniformed soldier. "Oh! There's Louis Quatorze!" she cried excitedly.

Though General de Gaulle, whom Jacqueline most admires, is very much of the twentieth century, his grandeur of person and august turn of prose are reminiscent of eighteenth-century glory. The First Lady, who has read all the general's memoirs in French, terms him the only person she can imagine being completely incorruptible. She thinks of the general as he thinks of France. And of all the myriad messages congratulating her husband on his election, General de Gaulle's was the most treasured. She asked for the cable to keep as her own.

It read: "Bienvenue cher partenaire! Avec mes amicales felicitations, je vous adresse, au nom de la France, tous mes voeux pour les États-Unis." Others tried to sum up the happy event in many words, but none, the First Lady believes, achieved comprehension with such grace and distinction as did the general in three, "Welcome, dear partner."

Winston Churchill is one of the President's heroes. He admires Sir Winston inordinately as a man of letters and

From this nursery, in the Kennedy's Georgetown house, Caroline Kennedy's rocking horse was moved to the White House.
(© JACQUES LOWE)

has read every written Churchillian word. He has also savored General de Gaulle's memoirs in English translation. They made such an indelible impression that in January 1960, when Senator Kennedy announced his candidacy for the presidency, he modeled part of his statement on the French Chief of State's opening lines:

Toute ma vie je suis fait une certaine idée de la France. Le sentiment me l'inspire aussi bien que la raison. (All my life I have had a certain image of France. This is inspired by sentiment as much as by reason.) Ce qu'il y a, en moi, d'affectif, imagine naturellement la France, telle une princesse des contes ou la madone aux fresques des murs, comme vouée a une destine éminente et exceptionelle. (My emotional side tends to imagine France like a fairy-tale princess or a frescoed madonna, dedicated to an exalted and exceptional destiny.) J'ai d'instinct, l'impression que la Providence l'a crée pour des succès achevés ou des malheurs exemplaires. (I instinctively feel that providence has created her either for complete success or utter misfortune.)

The final part of Senator Kennedy's statement read:

For eighteen years I have been in the service of the United States, first as a naval officer in the Pacific during World War II and for the past fourteen years as a member of Congress. In the last twenty years I have traveled in nearly every continent and country—from Leningrad to Saigon, from Bucharest to Lima. From all this I have developed an image of America as fulfilling a noble and historic role as the defender of freedom in a time of maximum peril—and of the American people as confident, courageous and persevering. It is with this image that I begin this campaign.

Baby John on his christening day, wearing his father's dress. Less than two months later, John F. Kennedy, Jr., arrived at the White House "nine-and-a-half pounds thin and long." (UNITED PRESS INTERNATIONAL)

Shortly before noon on January 20, 1961, the President-elect and Mrs. John Fitzgerald Kennedy crossed the White House threshold for the first time together. They stopped en route to the Inaugural ceremony at the Capitol. The President-elect and his wife left their own limousine at the White House, he to join President Eisenhower for the ride down Pennsylvania Avenue, while Jacqueline and Mamie Eisenhower followed in a second car. They were to return after the splendid ceremony and a following luncheon in the old Senate chamber of the Capitol as the thirty-fifth President of the United States and the thirty-first First Lady.

At 12:15, fifteen minutes after the new President had been sworn in, personal suitcases, Caroline Kennedy's rocking horse and, wrapped in protecting plastic, the First Lady's white-satin-and-chiffon Inaugural gown were brought into the White House. A few days later some of the choicest pieces of French furniture from the Kennedys' Georgetown house; paintings; books; and baby John's white wicker, pink-ribbon-run, dotted-swiss-swathed bassinet arrived.

Thirty-one years before this same bassinet had been painted beige and elaborately beruffled in peachy point d'esprit. In it then, wide-eyed, grave, with a fluff of faintly curling black hair, had lain a placid infant named Jacqueline Lee Bouvier. Its new occupant—nine and a half pounds thin and long—had had a hard time getting born. He is the newest, most beloved symbol of the New Frontier.

Epilogue

ON INAUGURAL DAY, as Jacqueline Kennedy entered the White House with her husband, the thirty-fifth President of the United States, another phase of her youth had ended. Now, the third youngest First Lady in the nation's history, she was to act as chatelaine of the most spotlighted home in all the land and carry on her responsibilities with grace.

Mrs. Kennedy was to bring her own unusual quality to the White House, a quality of youthful beauty, penetrating intelligence, and impeccable taste. She was to bring, too, a fantastic memory, a will to work, and a sense of value which instinctively rejects the meretricious; all traits indispensible to a successful First Lady.

Her passionate interest in literature, poetry, and the livelier arts was to encourage the mounting surge of American culture. Through her sense of history and love for beautiful houses, she was to make the White House a true museum. Always an imaginative hostess, Mrs. Kennedy's knowledge of three languages was to prove an invaluable asset in the entertainment of foreign visitors. On trips abroad she was to make friends everywhere.

Though public interest would follow her every move, the First Lady was to retain a core of privacy which would enable both the President and herself to relax and be replenished. Here, in this shelter, she fulfills to her own satisfaction her primary roles of wife and mother.

Mrs. Kennedy's special qualities, enhanced by experience in the years ahead, will continue to benefit her husband, her children, and the nation.

CPSIA information can be obtained
at www.ICGtesting.com
Printed in the USA
BVHW011956271221
624950BV00014B/680